The Crime Game

Michael Laver

The Crime Game

MARTIN ROBERTSON · OXFORD

First published in 1982 by Martin Robertson & Company Ltd,
108 Cowley Road, Oxford OX4 1JF

British Library Cataloguing in Publication Data

Laver, Michael
 The crime game
 1. Crime and criminals
 I. Title
 364   HV6030

ISBN 0-85520-561-X
ISBN 0-85520-562-8 Pbk

Typeset by Getset (BTS) Ltd, Eynsham, Oxford
Printed and bound in Great Britain
by Billings, Worcester

Contents

Opening

It would be no trouble at all for me to crack your head open with an iron bar and take all of your money. I've an iron bar with me, and the money would come in handy. If I decide to go ahead and do it, you won't have much of a say in the matter. You'll be lying on your back with a cracked head and no money.

If I want a little more cash than you are likely to have in your pockets, I can easily saw the barrels off my old shotgun and buy a Richard Nixon mask from my local surplus store. Then I could rob a bank. Nothing would be simpler. All I have to do is walk in, insert the sawn-off shotgun into the mouth of a cashier, pull back the firing hammers and ask for all the money. If this doesn't flush out the cash, I can pull the triggers and take it anyway.

Bank robbery may not appeal to me as a profession if I am on the squeamish side and I hate blood and guts. In this case I could swindle you. I could paint my own Picassos and sell them to you for huge sums. I could bounce cheques, reprogram the computer or sell the Eiffel Tower several times to rich morons.

There are several million ways of taking money by force or stealth, and I am not going to talk about a single one of them in this book. I am going to talk about how to get people to *give* you money.

People being what they are, very few of them will want to give you money. Those who part with the cash will often do so reluctantly and with a bad grace. Who cares? However much they might *wish* they didn't want to, they'll give you the money when they could just as easily keep it for themselves. They'll *want* to give it to you because you've made them an offer they can't refuse. Having people give you money is good enough, but it's not the best part. The best part is that, having given you all of their money, your victims will usually want to keep the forces of justice in the dark about what has happened. They will be reticent despite the fact that the forces of justice (the cops, the lawyers, the judges and the entire law-enforcement industry) would be only too keen to take an interest in your activities should they come to light. How much more satisfactory all this is than robbing banks or cracking heads, when the victim and the police are liable to gang up in their vindictive determination to put the robber behind bars. The best thing of all about blackmail, for example, is that the victim is usually just as shy of meeting policemen as the blackmailer.

Now for the bad news. At least when I crack your head open with an iron bar, I get all of your money right away. I can walk away from your bleeding body straight into the nearest store and spend the cash on whatever I want. When I rob a bank I've got suitcases full of money, and the only complication I face is getting them to a nice quiet spot where I can spend the cash in peace. On the other hand, when I kidnap your baby son, all I have is your baby son. I certainly can't go and spend him. The little person is no good to me at all unless I can use him to make you want to give me some money. I can hit you over the head with him, but an iron bar would be both more effective and more convenient. The best way of using him is for me to threaten to damage him severely if cash in large quantities isn't immediately forthcoming. I make this offer. You don't have to respond. You can sit on your hands and make no move at all, or you can pay me. If you don't make a move, I'm not *forced* to carry out my threat. I can back down and release your baby son anyway. Or I can kill him. I make an offer; you move; I move.

What follows is about how to make these moves and offers to maximum effect. I don't want to take sides, just to lay out the options. Taking sides is the easy part. Victims will wish that most of the things described in this book didn't happen. They can wish and wish, but they won't wish them away. When they kidnap John junior and threaten to kill him, you can always go to bed and hope that things will sort themselves out by the morning. This is, after all, an extremely popular method of fixing broken motor cars. As a method of resolving kidnaps it will be just about as effective. When the worst happens you might as well do things properly. This means considering all of the options and choosing between them. When you consider *all* of the options, some of them will look pretty nasty. It may make you feel quite brutal even to look at them, but shutting your eyes won't make them any nicer. When John junior is kidnapped, for example, one of the options is not paying the kidnapper and risking your son's death. Nothing can change the fact that this option is available, even if you never intend to choose it. Think yourself into the mind of your opponent. If *you* kidnap JJ and his pa doesn't pay, you *could* kill him. You may decide not to, but that doesn't stop infanticide from sitting there on the agenda.

On the other end of the phone line, those people who are considering indulging in extortion, blackmail or kidnapping need to know what is involved. What follows may well discourage many of them. It usually turns out to be the case that a person must really be prepared to carry out a threat before it's worthwhile making it in the first place. Flippant extortionists need, of course, to be discouraged, and this book should serve that purpose. Hard-nosed operators who *are* prepared to kill people will have considered the options already.

I shall insist throughout on treating life as a game. Some games, of course, are fun and can be played by people as a form of recreation and even as a way of getting away from things. Other games, such as poker and the games in this book, are deadly serious. Some of them are the things that people want to get away from. First, therefore, we need to be quite clear about what a game is.

A game is no more and no less than an interaction between

two or more people. It is an interaction in which each player plays a part in determining the result. Roulette, for example, is not a game. It is a mechanical way of losing one chip for every thirty-six that you bet. Poker, on the other hand, is one of the best games in the world. Who wins what at poker is decided by who makes which moves. In the long run, every player loses to the bank at roulette. In the long run, the best poker player wins the most money.

One frequent source of confusion is that not everyone who is affected by a game is one of the players. Say, for example, I have been hired to kill you because you have been rather slow in settling certain debts. I decide to run you over, and steal a fast and sturdy car to do the job. I eventually find you on a pedestrian crossing, but you spot me a half-second too soon. In an exquisite little moment which we will both remember for a long time, you have to decide whether to jump right, to jump left, or to stay still. I have to decide whether to swerve left, to swerve right, or to blaze straight on through. We're playing a game. The outcome is determined by the interaction of our decisions. You might get killed; you might survive. I might get paid; I might not. *We*, and only we, are the players. Say I choose to swerve right and I hit you head-on. This is going to leave a surprisingly large dent in the stolen car. The owner will not be pleased. The car owner is affected by the game, no doubt of that, but in no way can he be considered a player. The owner has no influence whatever on the result and can be ignored when we are trying to understand what will happen. All we need to do, in order to predict whether you live or die, is to process the choices that you and I are going to make in that poignant and decisive moment in which the game is played.

This means that when we look at kidnappings, sieges and hijackings, we won't consider the hostages. They're affected by the result, but they don't affect it. They are really the pawns in the game, and you don't find many good books on chess which spend too long on how a bishop's pawn feels about a queen's gambit accepted.

The great advantage of treating life as a game is that it

strips away most of the irrelevant detail. The kidnapper may have brown hair, blue eyes and a club foot. She may be a common-or-garden brown-eyed handsome man. That shouldn't make any difference when you are deciding whether to pay her or face her down. It doesn't matter whether it's Sunday or Monday, whether it's raining or sunny, night or day. What matters is the deal, and whether you are going to accept it. Of course, if her eyes are rolling around in their sockets and her ruby lips are flecked with foam, you have something to think about. (Not that foamy lips are here or there in the kidnapping stakes, unless you regard them as evidence that the kidnapper is mad. If you do, then you may make a different decision. On top of this, there is the problem that she may not really be mad. We'll be looking at the advantages of real or imaginary insanity at a later stage.) Games, therefore, give you the bare bones. They sum up the action.

There are, of course, games and games. Some games are all-out war, while true love is just as much a game as anything else. Most of life, not surprisingly, can be found between these two extremes.

Example: I want to steal all of your money.

I decide to ambush you on your way to work. As with all good ambushes, I decide to set it up really close to your house, right outside the door, in fact. The trouble is, you are in a house with two doors, a front one and a back one. *And* you have a fair idea that I may be waiting for you. This gives you two choices, to leave by the front or the back. It gives me two choices, to ambush the front or the back. If you come out of the door I've ambushed, I get all of your money. If you come out of a different door, I get nothing. (It's no good my trying to run around and catch you. You'd hear me coming and have time to unload both barrels of your sawn-off shotgun before I got to you. Too risky.)

What we have here, my friend, is a game of pure conflict.

Say that you're carrying a couple of grand. There are four possible outcomes:

I ambush

		Front door	Back door
Front door		+2000	0
		−2000	0
Back door		0	+2000
		0	−2000

You come out of

The back-door robbery game

If I ambush the door you come out of, front or back, I gain two grand and you lose it. (My gain is recorded in the top right-hand corner of the relevant box; your loss is in the bottom left.) If I ambush the other door, no money changes hands. Everything I gain you lose, and vice versa. For every outcome, the total of your payoff and mine is the same (in this case, zero). This constant sum is how a game of pure conflict can be spotted.

Two important properties of games of pure conflict relate to communication and to deals. If you and I each had CB radios and could talk to each other, we might have quite a lot to say. However, neither of us would believe a word that came out of the other's mouth. You tell me that you're planning to come out of the front door. I'm no wiser. I certainly can't assume that you're telling me the truth (whyever would you tell me the truth?).

I can't even assume that you're lying and whizz around to ambush you at the back door. That might be just what you wanted me to think. The game starts off with you liable to come out of either door. You tell me which door you're going to come out of. You still might come out of either door (unless you're *very* stupid), so our communication is irrelevant.

In the same way, we've nothing to do a deal over. We've

nothing to trade. The box in the diagram, known as a payoff matrix, sums the whole thing up.

Example: You and I get arrested after breaking into a bonded warehouse and stealing a lorry load of whisky.

The cops suspect us, but they can't prove a thing. We've worked out a cast-iron alibi ahead of time. We say that we were both drinking in the late-night Kalamazoo Club throughout the whole period that the robbery took place. They split us up and question us separately. They want to know all about this alibi. All of a sudden one of the detectives asks whether the Kalamazoo Club doorman was black or white. Now it's a pretty well mixed club, the Kalamazoo, and the doorman could be almost any colour. We didn't settle this when we fixed our alibi. One thing is certain: it would be a good idea if we both gave the same answer, but what should we say? I've not only got to think of what I say but also of what you are going to say. If we disagree on the doorman's colour, our alibi begins to fall apart. You are going to be asked the same question and will be trying to guess what I said. Do I say what I think, in the hope that you'll be trying to copy me? Do I say what I think you'll say, in case you don't. Do I say the doorman was black because I think you'll think that I'll think that you'll think . . . that I'll think that you'll think that the doorman might be black?

| | You say | |
	Black	White
I say Black	Freedom Freedom	Jail Jail
I say White	Jail Jail	Freedom Freedom

What colour was the doorman at the Kalamazoo Club?

What we have here is a game of pure co-operation. You might be tempted to think that co-operation doesn't make for much of a game. But if the players can't communicate properly, co-operation can be as tricky as conflict.

If we're allowed to talk to each other, the game disappears. Only *really* stupid policemen let suspects talk to each other in the middle of interrogations about their alibis.

Ambushes and alibis are at opposite ends of the scale. Most games are neither pure conflict nor pure co-operation but mix a little of both. Cast your mind back to the moment when I was trying to run you over for money. At first sight, that may seem like an interaction of pure conflict. You live or die; I get paid or not. But imagine that I'm a mercenary. In this case, there is also the chance that you could try to buy me off. If I'm getting five grand for killing you, you could always offer me ten to spare you. If we each had CB radios, we'd have quite a lot to talk about.

I

	Swerve right	Swerve left
Jump right	+5000 — Dead	0 — Alive
Jump left	0 — Alive	+5000 — Dead

You, me and that contract on your life

We can see straightaway that this is not a game of pure conflict, since the payoffs in each box don't add up to the same constant sum. Provided that you've got ten grand to play around with, outcomes which leave you alive are worth more *to both of us* than outcomes which leave you dead. You can give me ten grand not to kill you. *You're* happy to be alive, if ten grand poorer. *I'm* happy with a bigger payoff than I would get if I killed you. We have an incentive to co-operate.

All is not peace and love, however. I still have to keep up a credible threat to kill you, otherwise you will start to wonder why on earth you are giving me ten grand. This game mixes conflict and co-operation.

Mixed-motive games are where the fast action can be found. This is the sort of action involved in kidnapping, hijacking, extortion, sieges, blackmail and the whole family of occupations that put a premium on bargaining skill. This family of occupations is quite different from most other types of business activity. Robbery, fraud, murder and malicious wounding don't involve much interaction between the parties involved. Such interaction as there is tends to be travelling in one direction. Thus when I crack your head open with an iron bar, I can be said to have communicated with you, but you cannot really be said to have communicated with me. Our interaction is somewhat debased and lacking in richness. When, however, I blackmail you over some Polaroid pictures I happen to have discovered in your wallet, our interaction can reach a very high level indeed. This book is about mixed-motive crime, crime in which criminal and victim are forced to deal with each other and often share a very high level of common interest. Each needs to get along with an opponent who can't be trusted. The wheeling and dealing which result produce the politics of street life.

1

Extortion

THE SAD STORY OF THE RIVIERA LOUNGE

You're an honest nightclub owner with a nice little business lubricating dry throats in the Riviera Lounge. You never have any trouble that Henry the Hatchet can't handle, even if you like to take a walk while he handles it. One night you're buttering up some extremely stupid and wealthy customers when two insurance salesmen walk through the door; you usually butter insurance salesmen and eat them for breakfast, but you can see these two are going to stick in your craw. For openers, one stamps very hard on Henry's toe. This is a most unusual move to try out on someone the size of the Hatchet, and you watch with interest while your doorman's face turns grey-green. His feet must be nailed to the floor, since he makes no move when your new guests march straight across the bar in the direction of your office. They pay no attention at all to the comfort of any party who might be in their path. They clearly have some proposition on their minds. Your choice is emigrating or listening; you go to do business.

The deal is simple. They want to sell you some damage insurance. You feel pretty smug at having guessed their line of work and get over-confident. You settle back into your chrome-and-leather swivel chair and adopt the patronizing manner that works so well when giving insurance salesmen the bum's rush. You tell them you don't need damage insurance. You explain that Henry and his hatchet are 200 pounds of walking damage insurance. You like to think that even with nine good toes he will be able to hold his corner with the most excitable punter. At this stage in the conversation the salesman who broke Henry's toe in two places decides that he wants to make a point. He communicates this by grabbing the brass paper-knife laid neatly across your blotter and inserting it forcefully into the back of a hand. This is one of your hands, and you have carelessly left it on top of the desk. While you attempt to remove the paper-knife without getting blood on the rug, he produces a pistol and presses the barrel against the end of your nose.

His partner (the big one) is very patient. You now listen carefully while he explains the special features of their policy. It seems they are selling some brand-new type of prophylactic insurance. Such insurance, of course, is expensive, due to the vast expenditure on research and development which is necessary before any brand-new product can be marketed by a responsible organization. The special features, however, are well worth the extra cash. The new improved policy acts on the damage *before it takes place*! This is, of course, several hundred times better than old-fashioned policies, which pay you money only after the damage has been done and the punters have scarpered. The two salesmen are careful to explain that a lot of honest nightclub owners have recently been very sorry that they passed over such a wonderful deal. Very quickly nearly all of them suffered all sorts of damage. If only these people had taken out damage policies, they would have saved themselves a lot of money and aggravation. You are forced to agree that even in the Riviera Lounge damage seems to be on the up and up in the past half-hour. You decide to give the deal some thought. The nice salesmen give you ten minutes while they partake of free Harvey Wallbangers at the bar.

You are a realistic nightclub owner with a nice little business lubricating dry throats, and you know the score. You've got two choices: you pay or you don't pay. Your friends have two choices. They can hit the Riviera Lounge; they can leave it alone. That makes four things that might have happened by the end of the day. You can pay them, and they'll leave you alone. You can not pay them, and they'll hit the bar. These are the two sides of the deal you've just been offered. But you haven't got to be proprietor of a little goldmine like the Riviera Lounge by believing everything that people tell you. Your salesmen friends may just be two punks with a fake pistol, broad shoulders and a neat line in toe-crushing. After all, you are 95 per cent legitimate (almost). You could pick up the phone; you could call the cops, and you could have them run out of town. They *might* not be back, and they *might* have no friends. You would end up with a nice little business and all your money; no pay, no hit. *On the other hand*, those two may be psychos who get their fulfilment from smashing bars and like to make a little ready money on the side. You could pay them and they could hit you anyway. You will, of course, sue them for breach of contract, but that won't bring back the punters. You pay; they hit anyway. Neither of these two possibilities is in the deal, but life has taught you that insurance salesmen don't always say what they mean. So four things might happen — how do you feel about them?

The best you can hope for is no pay/no hit. That way you go to bed in the same state you woke up in this morning. This is not so wonderful, but it is better than the rest of the menu. The worst item is to pay these hoodlums and get hit anyway. This would be far from fair, but any punter with a magnifying glass and one of your price lists would be forced to admit that the liquid refreshment industry can be a little unfair at the best of times. Between heaven and hell comes the deal; pay/no hit or no pay/hit. Which is better? The price they're asking is pretty steep, but these two jackasses have done their homework. The Riviera Lounge is a classy joint. You've got a big investment in this place, and it earns you a living. Two runaway insurance salesmen could cost you a lot more in damage than they're charging for their prophylactic policy. They've got your number. The demand is set so that you prefer pay/no hit to no pay/hit. Just. You make a mental note to take a closer look at Henry's toe. It will make you feel a lot better to see that it really is smashed, since someone somewhere has been selling the inside dope. They could have asked you for anything. If they'd asked for more, you'd have called the cops and taken it on the chin. If they'd have asked for less, you'd have paid right up and felt pretty smug. But they didn't. These jokers aren't giving *anything* away. Already you've learned a very important lesson. Never, *ever*, let the bastards know what you're worth. Once you do, you're exposed; they're going to take you. If you have to give information away, make it look like you're having a hard time. That way if they take you, they won't take it all.

Eight minutes left and things look pretty bad. But you figure it through one more time. You pull out a pencil and start a doodle on your bloody blotter. You look again at those four possibilities.

		Them	
		No hit	Hit
You	Pay	2nd	4th
	No pay	1st	3rd

How you feel about damage insurance

Right away, the doodle makes things look rather different. If you look at your little problem like this it seems better not to pay *whatever the other guys do*. Don't pay. You get your first choice rather than your second if they don't hit you, and your third choice rather than your fourth if they do hit you. Of the two strategies you could choose, not paying is your dominant strategy, because it's the best thing to do whatever the opposition chooses. So why don't you just tell them to kiss off? Maybe this is making things a little too simple. Plenty of people seem to rub by pretty well in the damage insurance business. They can't all be dodos. There must be more to this than meets the eye.

Think again about the deal. The pitch is that they will hit

you if you don't pay and leave you alone if you do. The proposition was put more delicately than this but it amounts to the same thing. The only way to come out ahead is to figure out what the opposition is going to do. Once you can do this, you can work out the effect of paying or not. Your third choice may be better than your fourth, so you'd rather not pay if they hit you, but if paying makes them stop, this will give you your second choice, which is better still. Before you can make any sort of guess at how the big men in the bar see the world, you've got to decide just what sort of insurance salesmen they really are.

The two gentlemen may have just blown into town and be trying on a little stunt to help them raise some spending money. They may be hardened professionals who've been selling damage insurance since the day they learned to spit. There's always a chance that they're pure psychos who get a kick out of breaking things and don't care about the cash. These guys aren't in rags, however; they're in sharp suits. Either they're psychos with rich uncles or they make money somewhere along the line. You decide right away that they probably don't even have fathers, let alone uncles, but what you really need to know is whether damage insurance is their regular line of business. If they're freelances, they're going to be a whole lot easier to deal with than two professionals. Figure it through.

Every sales pitch is a one-off for a freelance salesman, who basically wants to take the money and run. A professional, on the other hand, sells damage insurance for a living. He needs to develop the damage market as a continuing source of income. Above all, a professional has his reputation to consider. While the freelance is delighted to sell any insurance at all, the professional must consider his image.

Take the freelance first. Heaven for the freelance is pay/no hit: all the cash, no aggravation. Hell is no pay/hit: all the aggravation, no cash. Between heaven and hell come pay/hit and no pay/no hit. Of course, no one would be selling damage insurance in the first place if he wasn't prepared to involve himself in a little rumpus in the cause of ready cash. You can be sure that pay/hit beats no pay/no hit hands down. Back to the blotter:

	Freelance salesman	
	No hit	Hit
Pay	1st	2nd
No pay	3rd	4th

(You on the left side)

Freelance salesman's world view

It doesn't take too long to work out that you've got a freelance beaten. A freelance has no incentive to hit, *whatever you do.* If you pay up, he gets his first choice rather than his second by *not* hitting you. If you don't pay, he gets his third choice rather than his fourth by backing down. You both have a dominant strategy, and this means that it doesn't even matter which of you moves first. You're better off not paying whatever he does. He's better off not hitting whatever you do. There's no point in either of you sitting tight to see which move the other makes. The game's over as soon as it's begun.

You can sum the whole thing up with a final doodle. Put the two sides together:

	Freelance salesman	
	No hit	Hit
Pay	1st / 2nd	2nd / 4th
No pay	3rd / 1st	4th / 3rd

You (bottom left) vs. the freelance salesman (top right)

No pay/no hit is the inevitable outcome. Whatever happens, you don't pay. Whatever happens, he doesn't hit. Even though a freelance salesman is no softie and has pay/hit as his second choice, he never gets the chance. You never pay. The freelance damage insurance salesman is a sorry spectacle. If all he wants to do is take the money and run, he'd better start running.

But what about the sharp suits these guys are wearing? They look like they're not short of paper money. They could be professionals. Such people have an important stock-in-trade, which they call *credibility*. They like respect, and they get respect because people believe what they say. People believe what they say because when a professional puts a little proposition to you, like breaking your legs if you don't do such-and-such or pulling your teeth out if you don't pay back the money he says you owe him, he tends to mean it. He is well-known to break legs and pull teeth in the course of a day's business.

So if these two young men are professional insurance salesmen with a reputation for straight dealing, they are going to regard no pay/no hit as just about the worst thing that can happen. If this goes on and the word gets around, they're going to lose a lot of respect and will be on Skid Row in next to no time.

Now for some good news. They're also going to be pretty goddam upset about hitting you when you've paid already. On the other side of every threat is a promise, and broken promises are apt to be as bad for business as empty threats. Why in the world would the owner of the Crystal Chandelier pay for damage insurance if the Riviera Lounge took out a policy and got hit anyway? Both no pay/no hit and pay/no hit mean a broken deal, and a professional takes his deals pretty seriously. (Pay/hit is not quite the end of the world. If a deal must be broken, it's just as well to have the money.) Hell for the professional is no pay/no hit. Heaven is pay/no hit. What could be better? He gets ready money, he gets respect, and he never has to lift a finger. This vision of heaven is, of course, why so many young men see damage insurance as an attractive line of work. It is a line of work which is not always a simple matter of going around looking tough and having people give you money, however. Sometimes a man can look tough, while his victim looks the other way. In such circumstances the pro salesman must do what must be done. Bones must be broken, teeth pulled and nightclubs wrecked before other clients begin to lose respect. All of this fits neatly on to the blotter:

	Professional	
	No hit	Hit
Pay	1st	3rd
No pay	4th	2nd

You

A pro racketeer and his Weltanschauung

While the freelance just wants some quick cash any which way, the pro is obsessed by enforcing the deal he offers. This deal is pay/no hit or no pay/hit. So if those guys at the bar are pros, what should you do? You are the same you as always and feel the same way as before. You sum up your little problem:

	Professional	
	No hit	Hit
Pay	1st / 2nd	3rd / 4th
No pay	4th / 1st	2nd / 3rd

You

You vs. a professional salesman

Don't go strutting around feeling good about your dominant strategy before you think it through. Sure, you are better off not paying, whatever Joey the Toe might do to you. But if the homicidal maniac is a pro, he's not going to make a move until you do. The move he does make is going to depend on whether you pay him or not. This is another way of saying that our friend doesn't have a dominant strategy. He's going to want to hit you if you don't pay him; he's going to want to be nice if you do.

If you think that's bad, hear this. You can't pussyfoot around with a pro. Well, you can try, but he knows that you have a dominant strategy; he knows that your dominant strategy is not paying. He's going to hit you; he's got no choice. (He doesn't hit you. You don't pay him. He loses a lot of respect.) The trouble is that no pay/hit leaves you both in a sorry state. You're both worse off than you would be with pay/no hit. What's more, *the game's in your hands*. You are the one who can *guarantee* pay/no hit by coughing up the ready money.

Nobody forces you to make the first move, and nobody forces you to pay. You want to move first because you want to pay. You want to pay because paying stops the pro from hitting you and because the pro has fixed your premium so that you would rather pay than suffer. As a matter of fact, you're rushing to pay as soon as possible. You want the salesmen to be 100 per cent certain that you're not tinkering with your no pay dominant strategy. As soon as they get even the faintest sniff of a dominant strategy, they're going to hit you faster than the speed of light just to keep their reputation in tip-top shape. That's why pro racketeers wear sharp suits. They make you feel grateful to be allowed to pay them money.

Four minutes left before Joe and Co. walk back into the room. You've pretty much decided to pay. There's just one other thing to think about. How about stalling? Not pussyfooting, just stalling. You spin some yarn about not having enough ready money right here in your pocket and needing a little more time. How might those gentlemen take a story like that? They will probably take it rather badly. The trouble is that they need you to make the first move if they are going to get their money. You stall. You don't positively *not* pay them, but you don't positively pay them either. They get jumpy. How do they know whether you just haven't paid yet or won't pay at all. There is a mighty fine line between the two. This is where the deadline they set comes into its own. For the next three and a half minutes you've not paid *yet*. After that, you won't have paid *at all*. In three minutes twenty seconds they'll start worrying about their respect. They'll take it out on the Riviera Lounge. The whole set-up is so goddam elegant it makes you want to weep. You go over to the safe and get out the money.

DR ENTERTAINMENTS HANGS TOUGH

Joe takes the money and goes. He is not particularly polite about it, considering that you have just made him rich. On the way out he asks if there isn't a short cut from the Riviera Lounge to the Crooked Bullet. Now the Crooked Bullet is owned by Danny Riordan, who is one of this city's most successful operators in the liquid refreshment industry. DR Entertainments not only owns the Crooked Bullet but also has a controlling interest in the Oasis, the Regency Suite and Danny's Place, not to mention a restaurant or two, as well as an establishment in which tired punters can relax in the company of sympathetic young ladies. Danny is not only a versatile and experienced host, but he is also an acquaintance of yours. He is apt to be grateful if you pass on some of the insights into damage insurance that you have picked up in the past half-hour. You give Joey the Toe and his partner some haphazard directions and turn back to the blotter.

DR Entertainments will be well-known to all the damage insurance salesmen in town. Danny runs around in an enormous black limousine. This comes complete with an enormous black chauffeur, who is an ex-heavyweight boxing champion of the world. DR Entertainments is big-league, and everyone would like to have them for a client. If Joey the Toe and his mouth get as far as selling Danny one of their fancy damage policies, he is going to be on a slippery slope and no mistake. Half the bad guys in this town, not to mention their kid brothers, are going to be inside a DR Entertainments outlet next day, waving bits of paper with 'damage insurance' written all over them.

DR Entertainments is what you might call a professional victim. Danny has a reputation to consider, just like any other professional. Taking out a damage policy the first time some sharp suit walks through the door is no way to protect a reputation. What's more, Danny has resources. Even if Joey the Toe comes back and breaks a few bones, even if this scares away punters from the Crooked Bullet (as a matter of fact, even if they *demolish* the Crooked Bullet), Riordan has the Oasis and a whole lot more to fall back on. They can wipe out the Crooked Bullet and show the world they mean what they say, but even damage insurance salesmen need some ready money to keep body and soul together. Breaking bones is a tiresome business if there's no profit in it. They may call it a day. Better still, other salesmen will take note that DR Entertainments hangs tough and is no easy mark.

All of this boils down to the fact that, unlike you, Danny is going to prefer no pay/hit to pay/no hit. He would rather take his medicine and build a reputation as a hard man. This will cut down on the number of nasty articles who will walk through his door in weeks to come, and will pay dividends in the long run:

		Salesmen	
		No hit	Hit
Danny (pro victim)	Pay	3rd	4th
	No pay	1st	2nd

Danny's preferences in his war with the salesmen

This means that if Joe and Co. are freelance, their run-in with Danny will look like this:

Joe & Co.

	No hit	Hit
Pay	1st 3rd	2nd 4th
No pay	3rd 1st	4th 2nd

Danny

DR Entertainments hangs tough

No problem. You didn't want to pay them even if they were freelance, and Danny will want to pay them even les. He guarantees his first or his second choice by not paying. The freelance is bound not to hit; after all, these are the same freelances who weren't going to hit you. No pay/no hit is a foregone conclusion.

If those guys are professionals, however, things hot up. The all-pro game looks like this:

Joe the Pro

	No hit	Hit
Pay	1st 3rd	3rd 4th
No pay	4th 1st	2nd 2nd

Danny

The all-pro game

When they played you, the pros sat tight and waited to see what you did. They'll do the same with Danny. They'd rather wait because they're going to hit him if he doesn't pay and leave him alone if he does. They don't have a dominant strategy. Danny, however, is at not at all like you. He has no incentive whatsoever to pay. You had a dominant strategy of not paying, but you still did better by paying if that made them leave you alone. Danny sees no pay as such a strongly dominant strategy (first and second choices) that the order of the moves is irrelevant. If he moves first, he's not going to pay. If he moves second, whatever they do, he's not going to pay. Danny just doesn't pay, and Joe the Pro hits him — no pay/hit.

Danny can't be dragged along into co-operating in the way that you were, and no one makes any money. Once this sorry state of affairs gets around, insurance salesmen are liable to give DR Entertainments a wide berth. No one who is anyone spends his life breaking bones for fun when they can be broken for cash at the Riviera Lounge.

CALLING THE COPS

When the dust settles and the hard men have gone home, you may wish that you had called the cops. Would it have made any difference? To figure this out you need to consider how the police feel about the world. Honest policemen want to beat criminals and prevent crime. When it comes to the protection game, they want to bankrupt damage insurance businesses both by making sure that the salesmen never get paid and by souring the whole commercial environment. This means that police preferences will be dominated by no pay outcomes. If they are forced to choose between no pay/no hit and no pay/hit, you can suppose that they would rather see the victim left alone than hit. Also, if the victim is going to pay anyway, they would probably rather see him left alone. You can see straightaway that while they always side with the victim, the cops only have *exactly* the same preferences as the professional. Now, once you call the cops, they usually take control; you lose your flexibility. We need to sort out whether you gain anything in exchange. You need to know what will happen after the cops are called before you can decide whether to pick up the phone.

Since the police have the same preferences as a professional

Police preferences are:

Racketeer

		No hit	Hit
Pay		3rd	4th
No pay		1st	2nd

You

Police view of the world of damage insurance

victim, the result is going to be no pay/no hit if you're dealing with a freelance and no pay/hit if you're dealing with a professional. When you face a freelance no pay/no hit is both what you most want and what is most likely to happen. Call the cops by all means. They may feel rather differently about the various things that might happen, but that doesn't really matter. Their intervention is going to guarantee your first-choice outcome. You might as well bring on the cavalry against those small-time chisellers and have them run out of town by experts.

The fun starts when you're up against a professional. We have already seen that the horrible beauty of a professional's game is that the victim has a big incentive to seize the first move. Worse, the first move he seizes is paying up. This result is not going to please the cops one little bit. They want to beat those guys more than you do. In fact, you don't really want to *beat* them at all, simply to come out losing as little as possible. When the chips are down, you'd rather pay the money and live in peace than sit tight and lose your club. You can control what happens by the way you move, and if you call the cops, you lose that control. Left to your own devices, you are going to settle on pay/no hit.

This means that you will decide not to call the cops. If you do call them, you'll be worse off than before. The cops have no chance of delivering no pay/no hit, your first choice.

You're getting pay/no hit, your second choice, without them. In fact, what they *are* going to deliver is no pay/hit and leave you worse off than before. The beautiful irony of the pro game is that not only do the salesmen have an incentive to keep the cops out of things, but the victim has this incentive too. What could be nicer than the enforced collaboration between salesman and victims that gives the professional villain his great strength? It sets up the offer you can't refuse and is the hallmark of this whole type of enterprise. Not only can the victim not refuse the offer but he has every incentive to protect the villain from the forces of law and order.

The professional victim, on the other hand, has *exactly* the same preferences as the police. The cops will always behave in the same way as the pro, who will not turn his nose up at the extra muscle. The police make the freelance victim nervous because they are prepared to sacrifice him for their greater cause. The pro victim is prepared to sacrifice himself, *this* time anyway, for his own greater cause, so he picks up the phone straight away.

We see that the police can speed things up when the action is pretty straightforward anyway, that is, with freelance salesmen and/or pro victims. However, they are no help at all in the one case in which the villain is likely to make money, the freelance victim facing the professional protection person.

THE CITY CLUB-OWNERS' MUTUAL AID SOCIETY

If the cops are no use, what else can you do? DR Entertainments was in much better shape than the Riviera Lounge because they had a string of clubs and a reputation. Of course, you would like a string of clubs and a reputation too, but such things aren't that easy to come by. Your best hope is to get together with a few others in the same spot. All over the city there are businessmen like you who have no choice but to take out a damage policy when a professional salesman comes calling. Put them all together and you have a string of clubs and maybe even a reputation. So set yourself up as the chairperson of the City Club-Owners' Mutual Aid

Society. Get each member to agree to help compensate any other who pays the price for turning down damage insurance. That way every member could take on the preferences, and the bargaining strength, of a professional victim. The Society would be a professional victim. Each member would be prepared to turn down damage insurance provided that he was compensated by the Society for any damage that resulted. Would this work?

It would if it discouraged the salesmen. But the damage policy costs less than being hit, so if the number of demands and hits didn't go down, the Society would lose money. It would be cheaper to club together and pay the demands than to compensate for the hits. But the salesmen need to make money, and they don't make money by making hits. So if every member of the society took a hit on the chin each time a demand was made (and got paid by the others for his pains), the salesmen should start to look elsewhere or at least moderate their demands.

The fact is that a hard-headed pro salesman can make money even faced with a well organized mutual aid society. The cost of each demand, of course, is a product of the greed and skill of the salesman, although any half-way sensible salesman will keep the cost of the policy below the cost of being hit. Even if the victims organize, a tough protection merchant can make money if he is prepared to do one of two things. If he keeps hitting bars even after all the owners stop paying him, he may wear them down. If he reduces his demands, while continuing to hit bars, the owners may find it cheaper to pay than to resist. In fact, there is always a demand that is so low that it is not worth resisting, so the salesmen can always make *some* money.

If the protection merchant can keep up the number of bars he hits even when the owners are refusing to pay, he will need to chop his demand less while still offering a deal that is more profitable to accept than to resist. Perseverance in the face of resistance will be handsomely rewarded. In all of this the salesman is greatly assisted by one inescapable, and very useful, fact of life: it is much easier to cause damage than to

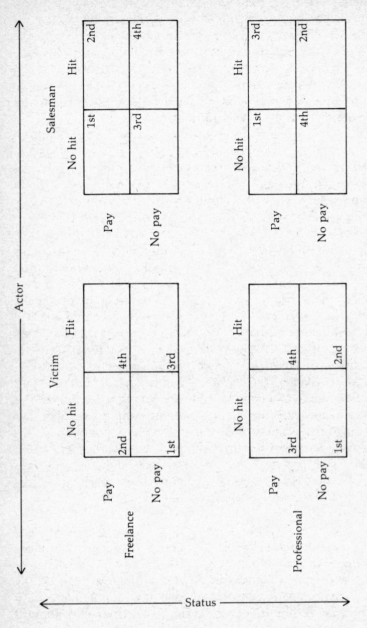

The Compleat and Unabridged Extortion Game

repair it. You can spend years building up your business. I can kick it to pieces in no time. This means that the City Club Owners' Mutual Aid Society will never totally defeat the protection salesmen. The main effect of the club owners' tight organization is to reduce the demands made of them to a point at which they are not worth resisting. There will always be some demand that is low enough to make resistance a bad bet.

From this we can turn back to the behaviour of the professional victim, since the City Club Owners' Mutual Aid Society is a sort of pro itself. Faced with the same demand as a freelance, the professional will prefer no pay/hit to pay/no hit. But a smart protection salesman can chop his demands low enough to reverse this preference. The salesman must have the resources and the inclination to continue hitting the victim in the face of resistance. Just how low the racketeer must go will depend on the relative resources of victim and villain and the costs of inflicting and suffering damage. When two hardened pros meet, we should expect the victim to be prepared to pay some low level of protection money, since damage is generally cheap to inflict and expensive to suffer. However, the cost will be considerably less than that paid by the freelance.

The City Club Owners' Mutual Aid Society works in the same way as the pro victim's reputation. It doesn't stamp out damage insurance, but it greatly reduces its cost. At the end of the day, one thing is clear: the salesmen should always make money if they're not too greedy. No one can stop the calculating professional.

THE COMPLEAT AND UNABRIDGED EXTORTION GAME

Two types of victim and two flavours of salesman make four different confrontations. One diagram sums them all up. Any of the four games we looked at can be assembled by introducing a salesman to a victim. The salesman will always be asking for just a little less than the cost of being hit. The most likely outcomes can also be handily summarized in a small table.

Salesman

	Freelance	Professional
Freelance	No pay/no hit	Pay/no hit
Professional	No pay/no hit	No pay/hit

Victim

How the protection game turns out

There is only one game that produces a payment (and no hit). This is the freelance victim versus the professional protection salesman. There is only one game, the all-pro version, that results in a hit (and no payment). You can see straightaway why protection salesmen are always professionals. The freelances have starved to death long ago. You can also see that these professionals make their money from freelance victims. Last, but by no means least, you can see why protection salesmen take a very dim view of any attempt by freelance victims to organize. The City Club Owners' Mutual Aid Society produces an all-pro interaction that is both tiresome and unprofitable. Before you put yourself up as chairperson, you'd better find out whether the men in sharp suits will want to buy you off or bump you off.

PASTURES NEW

Nightclub owners aren't the only people who need protection. Nearly every member of the business community likes to avoid damage and will pay to do so if the price is right. Prophylactic damage policies were designed for clients who don't like policemen, but, like all great discoveries, their potential is much greater than their original market. Everybody is doing it — though, as usual, you'll tend to hear about the failures.

Take, for example, the Safeway Poisoner. Sometime in May 1981 he injected three jars of food with Paraquat, a lethal weedkiller with no known antidote. He left the jars on the shelves of stores belonging to Safeway, the largest supermarket chain in the world. Shortly afterwards an unsigned and badly hand-written letter was received by Safeway, suggesting that half a million might clear the matter up. Here we have a lightly reworked version of the old protection game. The author in this case was certainly a freelance. The main evidence for this is neither the bad hand writing nor the lack of signature but the fact that anyone even heard about the demand in the first place. Despite some superficially attractive modifications added by the Poisoner to the old plot, Safeway was bound to win in the end, provided it kept its nerve.

Supermarkets are very vulnerable to this sort of operation, but this vulnerability is their bargaining strength. A huge chain like Safeway will lose millions very quickly if customers switch their business — and wouldn't you switch your business very quickly if there was even a whiff of Paraquat in the pickle? Faced with the prospect of all those fleeing customers, a mere 500 grand might seem cheap at the price. The answer, however, is that one does not find oneself in a position to take the decisions that matter to a chain like Safeway by being the sort of person who might fall for that one. The fact that the game is so easy and that supermarkets are so exposed means that the companies have little alternative but to resist. They are professional victims confronting a freelance extortion attempt. Resistance is both imperative and cheap. Not only does the chain have an overwhelming incentive not to pay, but the Poisoner has an overwhelming incentive not to carry out the threat. Sneaking around supermarkets trying to hide jars of poisoned pickle with no hope of reward is no way to make a living.

Quite simply, since both sides have a dominant strategy, the outcome is a foregone conclusion. *Whatever the Poisoner does*, Safeway should not pay. If its food is poisoned anyway, it suffers all the lost business plus the lost ransom if it pays, and 'only' the lost business if it doesn't. If the food isn't poisoned, it loses the ransom if it pays and nothing at all if it doesn't. Its decision is unaffected by what the Poisoner might do. What's more, its decision cannot itself affect the Poisoner's actions, since he too has a dominant strategy. If Safeway pays, there is no point in poisoning the food. The added risk brings in no extra cash. If Safeway doesn't pay, there is no point in poisoning the food either. He is not going to make money anyway: why add extra risk? The interaction between Safeway and the Poisoner can easily be reconstructed from the Compleat and Unabridged Extortion Game:

	Safeway Poisoner (freelance)	
	No poison	Poison
Safeway (pro victim) Pay	1st 3rd	2nd 4th
No pay	3rd 1st	4th 2nd

Safeway and its Poisoner

If the Safeway Poisoner is rational, he won't put Paraquat in the pickle. If he's not rational, there's no guarantee that paying will stop him. Both sides have a dominant strategy, so the order in which they move makes no difference to the outcome. Since Safeway has the outcome no pay/no poison at the top of its list, it has no incentive to exclude the police. All in all, the Safeway Poisoner can be awarded a few marks for a nice try. He may have the satisfaction of a front-page story in a national tabloid but cannot expect much more out of a freelance extortion attempt against a professional victim like Safeway.

This suggests that if food poisoning appeals to you as a line of work, you'd better do it differently. First, set up a company called the Friendly Food Protection Company. Make it a big company, and concentrate on small clients. Your product line, of course, is *poisoned food insurance*. You should by now have a good idea of what to do. First of all, you slip into a potential client's store and poison a jar or two of pickle. This is the only dangerous part of the whole enterprise. The best thing to do is to buy the jars there, take them home, poison them and then slip them back on the shelves. Most small shopkeepers spend their day concentrating on people who are trying to *remove* things. You then wander in, disguised as an insurance salesman, and offer a poisoned food policy.

The store owner is likely to be surprised, if not sceptical. This is where your two most telling arguments come into play. Point 1: your insurance, unlike ordinary poisoned food policies on the market, has a unique prophylactic quality. Point 2: your client already has a jar of poisoned pickle languishing dangerously on his shelves. If point 2 falls on disbelieving ears, you can suggest that he feeds the jar to his dog. Come back the next day (you can use the evening to do a little research on his business and fix the price of the policy). You won't get as much as Safeway would pay if it did pay (but it won't). Don't feel that you are not a big-time operator just because your clients are small shopkeepers. People make millions selling things to the keepers of small shops. You are peddling peace of mind, which is much cheaper to produce than all those tiresome consumer products, yet every bit as valuable.

Even if you've never poisoned a single piece of food in your whole life, you may already have tried another modest variation on the Extortion Game. How many times have you bought a loaf of bread from a large and reputable bakery, only to find a piece of rat shit, a toenail or some such revolting object nestling between the slices? You probably felt like demanding some compensation and wanted more than another sliced loaf baked from God knows what in recompense for all the mental distress involved in such a discovery. You write the bakery a pretty stiff letter. They ignore it. You write another, replete with dark hints about lawyers, consumer courts and the like. You're after a little cash to help you get over the shock. You probably don't see this as extortion through the mists of self-righteous indigestion. You think you *deserve* some compensation, and maybe you do. But that doesn't make the game any different.

You're a freelance extortionist trying to squeeze some ready money out of a professional victim. Do you have any chance of success?

Your basic threat is to damage the bakery business with a well publicized legal action against it. In the course of this, those customers who feel squeamish about eating rat shit or toenails will decide to buy their bread elsewhere. You would be just another Safeway Poisoner if you were asking for half a million. (OK, OK, I know you didn't put the shit in the sliced loaf, but your thinly veiled threat has just the same effect as his.) If you did ask for 500 grand, the bakery would throw your letter straight in the slicing machine. After all, it can't go around paying out that sort of money every time it makes an honest mistake, even if the lost business arising from one public court case would cost it even more. What you're looking for is a much more modest sum, just a hundred or so to make you feel better. You're making a demand that is so low that even a professional victim may be prepared to pay because the long-term benefits of hanging tough aren't worth the short-term costs.

All of which sounds very plausible, but I'm sorry to say that you're not going to make it on your own. Go back to the original extortion game. This time you're the freelance racketeer. You've two choices: to fight the bakery or not. It's got two choices: to pay you or not.

You'd love it to pay up without a fight — which petty criminal wouldn't? You'd hate to fight it for nothing.

		You	
		No fight	Fight
Bakery	Pay	1st / 2nd	2nd / 4th
	No pay	3rd / 1st	4th / 3rd

You vs. the bakery in the case of the revolting sliced loaf

Between heaven and hell, you'd rather fight and win (with costs) than not fight and get nothing. In other words, your dominant strategy is not fighting. You prefer this whatever the bakery does, and your position is identical to that of the Safeway Poisoner. Because you've been so modest, the bakery is in a different position from Safeway. Heaven and hell are still no pay/no fight and pay/fight respectively, but it would prefer to pay up without a fight rather than fight and win. But you're still going to lose, because no pay is still a dominant strategy for the bakery. It gets its first choice rather than its second if you don't fight, and its third choice rather than its fourth if you do. Most important, it knows you have a dominant strategy too. It has no incentive to get in there with a quick settlement because it *knows* that you're not going to fight. Whatever it does, it's not going to pay you — even a little bit.

Dropping the demand switches around the bakery's second and third choices and might look like a good idea at the time, but it doesn't change the outcome. The simple fact is that the freelance extortionist always loses, whoever the victim and whatever the demand.

Your only hope is to call in the professionals, or at the very least to threaten to call them in. Consumer protection agencies have a reputation for taking on companies in cases like this. If they did not take them on and did not win, they would be a joke. *Now* we see some hope of getting paid. Going back to the original story, you'll remember that a pro racketeer can squeeze a little bit out of a pro victim if his demand is modest. The consumer protection agency, like the pro racketeer, has no dominant strategy; it'll fight or not depending on whether the bakery pays. This means that the bakery will pay if the demand is kept low enough. Just like the pro racketeer, the consumer protection agency is looking for a fight or two to boost its reputation. It doesn't feel too bad about fighting and losing, since every time it stands up and fights, the action does it some good. This doesn't mean, however, that it can pull off making big demands of pro victims.

PUT IT ALL TOGETHER AND WHAT DO YOU GET?

A successful extortion demand is marked out by the way it makes the victim and the author want to co-operate. This co-operation shows up in three basic ways. The first, and most obvious, is that the victim wants to give the author money. Such an unusual desire is what makes life so simple for the recipient and extortion so much more convenient than old-fashioned robbery. Most victims have to be prised forcibly from their money, and this not only causes undue aggravation but also means that any incident runs the risk of escalating into a serious wounding or a murder. The desire of the extortion victim to pay up is a direct result of the demand's being lower than the cost of ignoring it. Both factors are within the control of the author of the demand and must be manipulated with calculated restraint.

The second remarkable feature of the extortion game is the way in which certain victims can be forced to make moves that are not consistent with their dominant strategies. When each player has a move that is better, regardless of the move made by the other (*both* have dominant strategies), then the result is a foregone conclusion, and the order in which they move makes no difference. When one player has a dominant strategy and the other doesn't, it must be the case that the latter's best move depends on the move chosen by the former. In those circumstances the player with no dominant strategy prefers to wait and see. Things can be set up, as in the case of the professional protection salesman and the freelance victim, so that the victim is better off moving first and not playing his dominant strategy. This may seem a rather esoteric point, but it explains why extortion victims often seem to act against their own best interests.

The third special advantage enjoyed by some forms of extortion is the disinclination of some victims to call the cops. This flows from the desire of the victim to pay and to move first and is, of course, extremely convenient. All in all, a professional operator working on a freelance victim is taking candy from a baby. Anything else is a waste of time.

2

Threats

THE SHOWDOWN

If you (yes, you sitting there reading this) don't get off your butt and send me two grand, I'm going to tear off your head and feed it face-first into a sausage machine. You don't believe me? Maybe you think I don't have a big enough sausage machine or a strong enough stomach? Maybe you should try me.

Let's broaden our horizons a little. We can't all be professional damage insurers, but we can all make a threat or two when the need arises. Everyone makes threats, even if some people like to think of them as promises. Because there's nothing more pathetic than an empty threat, we need to be very careful. Because there's nothing more profitable than one that scares your opponent half to death, anyone who wants to make his way in the world must perfect the art.

The best way to get to the heart of the problem is to take a very simple example. Don't think I've forgotten about the two grand you owe me, but say, for the sake of argument, I take you and some other joker on one side and offer the pair of you the free gift of a straight hundred if you can agree on how to divide it up. If you can't, you get nothing. I'm a malevolent philanthropist with a pile of money, and I'm going to make the same offer time and time again until I get bored. What happens?

Now you and the Joker are about the same size. You might think that since there's nothing to choose between the pair of you in the strong-arm stakes, you'll each end up with half of the cash. But what if your buddy announces in the first game that she wants ninety-five out of each hundred that's on offer,

35

and she makes it clear that if she doesn't get the ninety-five, no one gets anything? You can try preaching a little sermon on fairness or some such irrelevant nonsense, but if she doesn't listen (and who would?), you've still got to decide what to do. Do you stand up or back down?

It might be that this is not the only game the lady's playing. Maybe another philanthropist is waiting in the wings with an even bigger wad. She might have been offered ninety as an advance payment just to play the rival game, on condition that she plays no other. She comes to you and tells you that unless you cover the ninety and then some more, she's not going to deal. If no one is running around offering you money, there's not much you can do. She might be lying (we'll talk about that later), but if she can prove she's not, you should be thankful to walk away with as much as five.

This is not a very interesting threat, if it is a threat at all. It's more a declaration of intent. Any opponent who has her head on straight will certainly do something that gives her more money than the *status quo*; there's no point in even trying to argue. She tells you: 'I do indeed have my head on straight, and if you don't give me a better deal, I'm going somewhere where I already have a better deal.' Students of English grammar will note that this declaration has the structure of a threat ('if you. . .then I. . . .'). It's sort of a threat, to be sure, but it's not going to set the world on fire. 'If you don't give me ninety-five, there's someone next door who'll be happy to oblige' is more a statement pointing out the facts of life to a reluctant opponent than one setting any sort of strategic problem. I'll call it a *boring* threat. It's not one of those lipsmackin', fingerlickin', downhome threats that's going to make her a millionaire. After all, what happens when there's no one next door?

Of course, when there is a whole cluster of boring threats on the table, made by both sides, it can take some pretty fancy footwork to sort out who gets what. I'm not saying that you don't have to be smart to come out ahead; I'm saying there's not much action around. To get very rich, you need to make what I like to think of as *real* threats. A real threat is one you'd rather not have to carry out, one you might not even be able to carry out.

Forget the rival philanthropist and return to the original game. The two players share the kitty if they agree on how to divide it and share nothing if they can't. Now, simply staying alive costs a lot of cash these days. Every time you get nothing, you're bleeding to death. Your hard-nosed opponent goes on demanding ninety-five out of each hundred, and threatens to let you both bleed if she's not accommodated. You can't stomach this and refuse to co-operate. No one gets anything.

Forget fairness. We have here a problem of pure strategy. If the game was played only once, you could call her bluff. You know she has no reason to blow the whole works if she doesn't get what she wants. It would just be downright spiteful to let you both bleed if you can't agree, and nobody ever got rich simply by being spiteful. But if the game is played over and over, things are very different. She needs to consider all of the threats she wants to make in the future. She might carry out this one in order to gain your respect. You both lose this time, but she gains next time because you listen more carefully. Now she is making a real threat. Both she and you will be worse off if she has to carry it out.

This brings us to the heart of the matter, *credibility*. In a one-off confrontation a threat to do something that makes you worse off than you were before is *incredible*. Why would you ever carry it out? When the confrontation is to be repeated over and over again, the same threat must be taken very seriously. In the first place, you may carry out the threat, at a loss, to enhance your credibility. This amounts to spending a little today in order to buy the psychological muscle that makes you money tomorrow. You're doing exactly the same thing as a bank robber who forks out a grand or so for the heavy machine pistol that makes life so much simpler when he wants people to give him all of their money. Of course, you would like someone to give you the heavy machine pistol for Christmas, but in a hard world you have to spend money to make money. The loss you suffer today, when you carry out a real threat and do yourself an injury, is an *investment*.

Much more important, if you want to get rich threatening people, every threat you make puts your credibility on the line. And the person you threaten knows that your credibility is on the line. When you make a threat and then back down, people stop listening to you. This means that as soon as you make a threat, you have an incentive to carry it out. You may be forced to carry it out to retain the respect you have so carefully built up, even if this costs you in the short term. When you make a real threat, you make a gamble. You stake some credibility in the hope of winning more. Before the threat is made, all things may be equal. Once you have made it, things will never be quite the same.

If you want to get a feel for this, take yourself back to school. Young children and hoodlums are better than most of us at handling the notion of respect. Think of the teachers you respected way back in the best years of your life. I'll bet you a straight fifty that they were the ones who hardly ever made threats because they hardly ever had to. And they hardly ever had to because they carried out the threats that they did make. Think of the teachers you despised. They were the pathetic ones who were always making empty threats, then finding any excuse to back down. The reason we have such a discipline problem in our schools today is that they don't teach teachers how to threaten any more.

It's the same thing when you borrow money. Think of the times you've borrowed money and forgotten to pay it back. Some people just ask to be forgotten. Say, however, that you're borrowing money to set up an expensive robbery. Your local bank will probably not lend against such a venture, however soundly you have costed it, and even if it is bound to be a sure-fire success. You will either have to tell fibs about wanting to build an extension to your home, or you will have to raise the cash elsewhere. You will need to go to a very serious person who is going to break your legs in several places if you are a day late or a penny short with the repayment. If you are two days late, he is going to kill you.

And it's no good contemplating life in a wheelchair, smugly certain that he won't kill you because he'll have no hope of getting his money then. He's not going to kill you for your money. He's going to do it for *other people's* money, for all the money they will pay back right on schedule when they see what he has done to you. As a matter of fact, he's looking for one or two people to kill in order to make sure the others stay in line. The only thing that stands between someone who bankrolls robberies and the breadline is respect, credibility.

So what do we know about credibility? First, consider *resources*. As any poker player knows, it's a lot easier to win if you have a bigger stake than your opponent, especially since just staying alive costs money as we have noted. You can be sitting tight on two nice pairs and knowing you have everyone else beaten into a cocked hat. Big deal: it won't stop the millionaire in the opposite seat from raising the limit and making it just too expensive to see what he's got. You lose anyway, even if he's holding a busted flush and not even an ace up his sleeve. To him that hath shall it be given, if all that it takes to win is to outlast the opposition in a head-on confrontation. When you make a threat that costs you both money if you have to carry it out, that threat is much more credible if you have more resources than the other guy.

Here we face our first big problem. You know how much *you* have but not how much *she* has. *She* knows how much she has but not how much *you* have. Now we'll take our first trip around a hall of mirrors that we'll be visiting again. Even if you know what she's got, does she know you know? Do you know she knows you know? Does she know you know she knows you know she knows? (And then some more.) All of these things are important, though you can call it a day when your brain starts to hurt.

If *everyone* knows *everything*, there is no point in the poorer player putting up a fight in the first place. He is bound to bleed to death in a showdown. In this case, the rich player can clear the whole kitty, minus only whatever is necessary to keep the poor player alive and playing. Your fancy friend demands ninety-five out of every hundred, every time. She has more cash than you to start with. If you don't back down, you bleed to death before she does. Shortly before you bleed to death, you are going to agree to take the five, assuming that it's enough to keep you alive. Since you know that you're going to have to take the five in the end, you might as well take it straightaway and not waste money finding out what you already know.

This is the old story of the smart capitalist and the disorganized worker. Sure, the worker can threaten to strike, but he is going to die of starvation before the capitalist, and everyone knows this. The threat is incredible, and the worker has no bargaining power. The capitalist demands the whole kitty, minus only whatever is necessary to keep the worker alive and working. The beauty of all this is that if you've got more resources to start with, you don't even have to use them to beat a poorer opponent. Simply having them is enough. Just as long as every one knows you have him beaten, it'll never be worth taking you on.

That, of course, is the easy part. Things are much more complicated when no one is certain about who has what. A whole range of factors come into play, since you would obviously be crazy to take anything an opponent said at face value. Sorting what comes out of people's mouths into fact and fantasy is clearly more a matter of experience than anything else. Yet people also have to make moves from time to time, and these can give you much more useful information if you know how to decode it. *You* have to make moves too. Knowing that your opponent is trying to interpret these, you will be inclined to try to confuse her. You might have hardly a cent to your name and still come on strong, acting like a millionaire to frighten off the opposition. You may be a millionaire yourself but make your moves like a pauper to sucker the opposition into exposing itself for the kill.

If you want to make effective threats, you're torn between wanting to show your hand to scare off the opposition and wanting to conceal it in case it's better fixed than you are. Everyone else will be trying to do the same thing. The result is usually quite unpredictable. Sometimes you can take a hard-nosed position to convince your opponent that you've more resources than she has. If she believes that you can sustain bigger losses in a showdown, she may crack first and assume, mistakenly, that she is poorer. On the other hand, this ploy can backfire. She may be playing you along. If no one knows it all, then the poor *can* beat the rich. They beat them by playing richer than they are and by being believed.

So, your hard-nosed lady opponent demands ninety-five out of every hundred, thinking she's got the resources to grind you down and thinking that you know this. As it happens, you *do* have less than she, but you shake her up when you come right back and refuse to accept her deal. You ruin a few games by refusing to co-operate, and she starts to worry whether she's got things right. She may think that she has you beaten, but that you just don't realize this. She may worry that she is actually poorer than you are, that you've suckered her into thinking she is on top. Now things start to get really interesting. It may be that you are operating at a lower level of information or skill than she is, or it may be that you are better at the game. Either possibility could lead to your hard-nosed response. You might actually force her to back down even if you are poorer *and* more stupid (a phenomenon often referred to as beginners' luck). This is because an uninformed and unintelligent analysis of this sort of confrontation can often lead to the same conclusions as those of a maestro. Playing poker with a moron who has only just learned the rules is a dangerous experience, especially if you can't be absolutely certain that he *is* a moron.

This is only the beginning. For example, a rich player may declare his resources in order to scare off the other side and leave them both in no doubt who will win in the end. This cuts short any time-wasting and expensive showdown and brings forward the profit-making phase of the game (in which the weak players know their place). But what if you are being hustled? Your opponent may play in such a way as to make you think, mistakenly, that you have more resources and therefore reveal them. You hope to frighten off the opposition, but you merely open yourself up for the kill. Another hustler's ploy is to declare certain resources, as if these were the whole lot, and sucker someone into parting with all he has, only to discover he was beaten from the start. When someone puts his cash on the table, all that you can be sure of is that he's got *at least* that. You will never know what he may be hiding in his back pocket.

THE HUSTLE (NEVER SHOW YOUR TRUE SPEED)

The classic hustle, of course, is worked in pool halls. A good pool player selects a worse pool player and plays him for money. The sucker takes the bet because the hustler has been publicly playing far below his best performance, his true speed. The sucker thinks he will win. Of course, the hustler beats the sucker, but he *only just* beats him and makes his win look like the result of a lucky shot. This encourages the sucker to bet again and again and, to win his money back, maybe even to double up. And all the other potential suckers who may be watching will still think that the hustler is an easy touch. The sucker may win a little, lose a little, but at the end of the evening the hustler's 'luck' leaves him with most of the important points and nearly all of the sucker's money.

You are a very good pool player and want to make a living beating suckers. You set yourself up in the action room of a pool hall and start playing. You will need a lot of self-control because you must resist the temptation to show off and play at your best. You don't have to be the best player in the room to be the best hustler. You do need to be good enough to know who you can beat and by how much. When you set up your stall, however, you can't play like a complete dodo, or no one will take you seriously. If you try to sucker them into a game, for a moderate bet, and you beat them, they'll spot you for a hustler straightaway. You're never going to make enough money on a single game to retire. Each game sets up the next.

So you start playing. You look moderately good and probably a little cocky, the sort of person who fancies himself enough to make a little wager. You are looking for a sucker who really is the sort of person you're pretending to be. The action room is just the sort of place where these people hang out. Someone takes you on, and you make a little bet. Now, you can let him win or lose this particular game — it doesn't really matter. What matters is how you do it. Whatever happens, the result must look pretty close.

If you do win, win by a little bit and make the other player look good. This is not too difficult; it simply involves setting him up with one or two good breaks. You only just win. Given his good breaks, he feels that he will beat you in the long run. You can be pretty cocky about your victory, strutting around and generally getting up his nose, or you can play it cool, acknowledging your luck and only playing on 'against your better judgement'.

On the other hand, you can lose the first game. You can't guarantee that your opponent will have good luck, so you have to have bad luck. If you *just* miss one or two 'ambitious' shots, you can put on a good show of wanting another match, insulting your opponent's ability and getting up his nose this way. In the end, all that matters is that he keeps playing. Once he's playing, you're in business. You have to win sometimes, of course, otherwise you don't make any money. The important point is to win while leaving your opponent hope, and to organize the wins and losses in such a way that he is tempted into increasing the size of the bets. Upping the stakes may be his way of capitalizing on his 'easy' winnings or recouping his 'unlucky' losses. Once more, it doesn't matter, but the stakes must go up to make the hustle worthwhile. If all of this is done properly, the sucker goes home the poorer. He may complain about his luck, but he will never even suspect that he has been hustled.

All of this is pretty simple if you've got the knack. Moving on to greater things, you can start by letting the sucker get a faint idea of what he is up against. (When the sucker gets suspicious, you're halfway along the road to the most skilled and exciting occupation of them all, hustling hustlers.) A sucker may have seen you around without your realizing it and may know that you are better than you pretend. Someone may have pointed you out to him. You may have hustled him badly. Most probably, you have set things up to so that he starts to suspect you. If a sucker bets against you, knowing that you're hustling him, there can be only two reasons for it: The first is that he wants to lose money; the second is that he is trying to hustle you (this is very stupid of him, but conceit and greed drive people to do stupid things).

The usual form is for the sucker to ask you for a big handicap. He knows that you are playing below your best. He thinks he knows what your best is. He tries to squeeze a handicap out of you that more than compensates for the difference in skill. He feels pretty smug. This is the situation in which the fact that no one has any idea of your true speed is your biggest asset. You're good, and you can give all sorts of handicaps to suckers and still 'just' beat them. Having a big handicap squeezed out of you is one of the best hooks for getting a sucker on the line. If you give it too freely, he'll be suspicious. You have to let him think he's outwitted you. (In the cold light of day, anyone who thinks he has outwitted a genuine hustler needs a head examination, but in the heat of the moment such mistakes are easily made.) The bottom line, of course, is that the handicap changes nothing. You still retain a large enough winning margin to control the way the game goes. Everything we have already discussed still applies.

Conceit is such an overwhelming motivation for many people that letting a sucker think he's hustling you is much the most effective way of upping the stakes. You hustle your way into this delightful position by giving away a little 'too much' about your skill in the early stages. You win a little too easily and hustle a little too crudely. The sucker comes back arguing for a big handicap, which you reluctantly give him. Then you *really* have him. The only way you can go seriously wrong is by giving away a handicap that means that you have to show too much of your true speed in order to make a profit. It is better not to play at all than to do this. No single bet is worth showing your top skill to a sucker. The only time you do this is when you can retire on the proceeds.

The ultimate joy is to out-hustle another hustler. This, of course, is a high-risk operation, though in some ways hustlers are easier to hustle than anyone else. The easiest person to beat and to win big money from in the process, is the person who reckons he has you beaten. Hustlers usually think they have suckers beaten. This makes them vulnerable. The *real* action comes when two hustlers, who know each other to be hustlers, meet head on. Things can get very complicated. Neither knows the other's true speed. Each is going to play if he thinks he can get an edge. Both think that they have an edge, but only one really does. The perfect position to be in is to have your opponent beaten, to let him think that he has you beaten, that you think you have him beaten, that you think he thinks you think you have him beaten. . . and so on. The danger is that this is just what he would like you to think.

Pool hustlers, of course, don't threaten people in the course of hustling them. But threateners often hustle. In fact, any successful threatener *must* hustle if no one knows who is in the stronger position.

There is almost no limit to the finessing that can go on when no one knows your true speed. You have a chance however weak you are. After all, didn't you hire Henry the Hatchet to guard the door of the Riviera Lounge because he weighed 200 pounds and stood six foot three? Didn't you turn down the five-foot karate champion who ate cars for breakfast and killed bad guys with his little finger? Even though Henry is out of condition, the important thing is that he is big enough to scare off the opposition without having to move a muscle. You hire doormen to keep the peace, not to kill people. Big doormen keep the peace better than small ones. Small ones always get into rumbles because they have to keep proving they're tough. The Hatchet's top speed is about one mile an hour but no one ever dares to find that out.

So this is Important Lesson Number One in the threatening business. If you've got more of what it takes, make sure that the opposition knows. Then you won't even have to use what you've got. If you've got less of what it takes, play your cards close to your chest and act tough.

FOOLISH VIRGINS

Important Lesson Number Two has to do with how quickly you want the cash. The longer you can wait, the more you get. It's a funny thing, but most people think a wad in their pocket today feels better than the same wad, or even a bigger one, tomorrow. Say you are doing a little job for me, eliminating one or two minor enemies. I offer you five grand now or six next year. Even if inflation is only 1 per cent, you'd take the five grand now. After all, you might get eliminated yourself before next year, and you didn't become a hit man to save up for a ripe old age. But if I offer you five grand now or fifty next year, you might decide the fifty is worth waiting for. Just as everyone has his price, so everyone can trade off cash today against cash tomorrow. Just as everyone's price is different, so everyone discounts future cash flow in a different way.

Now, it might be that I need to pay you next year because the characters you are going to eliminate for me have wiped out my business by unfair competition and price cutting. I need a year to put together some cash. The COD price is five grand, which I don't have. I'll just have to keep upping what I pay next year until I find your trade-off point. You won't take six. How about seven, eight, nine, ten, fifteen. . .? It turns out you won't take fifteen, but you'll take twenty. This may seem a little extortionate when you would barely get 10 per cent interest on a savings account, but then if savings accounts were so attractive, you'd be in a different line of work. Of course, I can tout the deal around, and I may find someone who'll do the hit for a smaller payment next year. He would still have a five-grand COD price: this is the going rate. Maybe he would be prepared to take ten grand next year instead. He simply has a longer-term view of the world than you. He discounts future cash flow less and, of course, he gets my business.

If two people discount their future income differently, then they are going to approach the business of threatening from different angles. The one who wants the money quickly will be less concerned with credibility and respect, since respect is a way of guaranteeing future income. The one who is prepared to sit and wait is the one who wants his future threats to be credible. He sets greater store by being able to threaten people next year and the year after because he prizes the profits more highly. A foolish virgin who wants it all now can't expect to be taken seriously when threatening to do something that harms her now but enhances her future threatening power. Whoever is prepared to sit and wait is going to win. This is because once he makes a threat, he carries it out if he has to. If the opposition knows this, it may back down.

People who are prepared to sit and wait are often thought wiser than those who want their Cadillacs now. We see that indeed they are wiser, since it is they who inherit the earth. If two players start the game with the same wherewithal, the one who can wait for riches can demand a bigger share straightaway. Because she's prepared to wait, she can beat the opposition in a showdown, and as soon as the opposition realizes this, it caves in. This is one of the delicious ironies of threatening people. If you don't mind waiting, you get it now. If you want it now, you never get it.

This explains the power of the Sicilian Mafia, whose men of respect have fashioned the threat into its most perfect form. Everyone who needs to know can tell from the cold stare or the extravagant politeness that he is being threatened, and threatened good. They never have to spell it out. If you double-cross them over a cup of coffee, you're going to be very sorry. You may wait ten years to pay your dues, but you'll pay them because the notion of respect is part of the way of life of a *mafioso*. That's what makes him such a frightening opponent. He can wait; you're going to lose in the end; so what's the point in playing? Forget what they taught you in economics. It's the losers of this world who cut their losses. As soon as it gets around that you cut losses, you're going to be taken. Who's going to feel threatened by a loss-cutter who shrugs his shoulders and writes off a nice try the first time someone faces him down? You're playing this game not against any hidden hand, but against a pack of wolves who'll tear you to pieces at the first sign of weakness.

Put resources and respect together, and you see how the weak can have the strong for breakfast. The strong player beats her weak opponent because she can outlast him in a showdown, but a strong player who's not prepared to wait for the showdown may pack it in as soon as a weak but far-sighted opponent fights back. In straight politics the collapse of the old regime is often speeded up by the frightening knowledge that a resolute and patient revolutionary group is convinced that time is on its side and is prepared to play a waiting game. One of the corruptions of power is that far-sighted hard men degenerate into rich hedonists who want their pleasures here and now. That's the time for the patient paupers to take over. There's nothing like a Swiss bank account to make you want to cut and run when the going gets tough.

So if you're an up-and-coming young pimp with a small stable and big ideas, don't be scared by the fat cats. Big ideas beat a bank roll any day. You should see those guys as an opportunity, not a threat. Lean on them, and lean hard. Crack heads and break bones, but pick the ones with fat guts and shiny cars. They're the ones who want to live. The quiet men with shabby suits and big investments are going to kill you.

ONE MAN'S MEAT IS ANOTHER MAN'S CADILLAC (IT'S ALL MONEY)

Before we finish with threats, we've got to think about the way every penny in this world means something different to different people. Quite a few have only a penny or two to rub together. Take one away and they starve to death. They want those pennies pretty badly. One or two could fill super-tankers with pennies and are not going to notice the odd half-million if they go astray.

If we all valued each penny the same as every other, then

no one with any sense would ever take out an insurance policy or make a little wager. We all know that insurers and bookies live in fancy houses and wear sharp suits, so why do we play games with them when it's clear the odds are loaded against us? We do it because we value some pennies more than others. We would rather have a 0.00001 per cent chance of a million than the certainty of a single pound, even though our expectation in the first case is a measly ten pence. A million will change your life, while a pound buys a jar of instant coffee. And a new life is worth more than a million jars of instant coffee. In the same way, we take out personal liability insurance in case a slate should happen to slip off the roof and bisect a passer-by, even though we have never heard of such an unlikely event ever taking place. The policy is cheap and the potential losses huge, so it hardly seems worth *not* taking a policy out. The several hundred thousand we might have to pay out if our house suddenly leapt up and killed someone is much more than a hundred thousand times worse than the few pounds we pay to insure against this improbable circumstance. We know it's a bad bet, but it's worth it.

We make the insurers and bookies rich because a penny or two either way, when life is comfortable, doesn't make much difference, while millions either way make all the difference in the world. Some pennies, of course, are very valuable, particularly the ones that keep us from starving to death. We'll only swap one or two of those for several million of the ones that buy us mink coats and Cadillacs.

The experienced threatener can put all of this to very good use. Most people go through their lives thinking of a penny as a penny as a penny. You can make a lot of ready money by pointing out to them that they are wrong. They will then give you some of their worthless pennies in exchange for being allowed to keep the valuable ones. You don't mind. When you go off to buy your second Cadillac, one penny looks very much like any other.

You may remember that a few pages ago I threatened to tear your head off. This was a real threat, since it would have made both of us worse off if you had forced me to carry it out. I ran the risk of being apprehended by the forces of law and order. You probably thought of pointing this out, but I, hard man that I am, would simply have replied that I wouldn't be half as sorry as you would be when it was all over. You'd be running around looking stupid with no head. You'd have to decide whether it was better to run a tiny risk of something *very* nasty happening to you or to give me the two grand. (It's not that different from buying a fall-out shelter). And it's not as if it would have been your *last* two grand, which you might well have valued as much as your head.

The skill lies in guessing how much the victim values the particular bundle of money you want to relieve him of and in concealing how distasteful you will find it to tear off his head. Only you know this for certain, but the victim will be trying to work it out. This is the power of someone who doesn't mind dying. Since most people regard dying as one of the worst things that can happen to them, their fear can be exploited by those prepared to run big risks for huge profits or who really don't mind dying that much. If you know I've only three months to live when I threaten to tear your head off and if I look like I mean it, you'll be pretty goddam scared. You'll give me the money.

A few years ago Cunard received a phone call threatening to blow up the *Queen Elizabeth II*, which was then at sea loaded with passengers, if large sums of money weren't paid out to the caller. Cunard probably gets calls like this all the time. What made this one special was the fact that the bomb was to be set of by two terminal cancer patients who were on board. This twist in the plot was sufficient to frighten Cunard into a full-scale alert. While it says it didn't pay (and it probably didn't because we heard about the demand), it clearly came closer to paying than it does with most common-or-garden ransom demands.

While we can't all be terminal cancer patients, we can all cultivate a slightly crazy or obsessive air that lets people know we don't care about the same things they do. Most people think through their response to a threat by putting themselves in the threatener's shoes. Too often they decide that if they were doing the threatening, they wouldn't carry the threat out, so they don't pay. However you do it, you have to make sure that the victim knows that you don't think like him.

You can practise your technique on pedestrians. How many times, when you have been driving to an important business meeting, have you been held up by some smug pedestrian parading around on a crossing as if he owned the place? You've probably already tried scaring him, roaring up to the crossing and braking only at the last minute. But some of these suckers would make you want to vomit the way they walk right on, smirking about all the trouble you will be in if you knock them over. You've got to make them realize that you won't be in half as much trouble as they will if you hit the accelerator and leave a smirking heap of blood and bones behind you. Everyone does this differently, and the only way to perfect your technique is to practise. Keep trying until they run for cover as soon as you turn the corner.

Important Lesson Number Three: live like you don't care, and die rich.

SO WHAT?

Most of the rest of this book is about threatening people, one way or the other, to make a living. So you'd better get it right. If the cards are on the table, things are simple. The rich and far-sighted are going to threaten their way to even greater riches. No one can beat them. The poor can beat the rich if they're prepared to wait long enough in a showdown. The men of respect beat the punks.

When nobody knows what's what, you've got to guess. Whatever you do, act like you need respect, like you're rich and like you're far-sighted. Of these qualities, respect is the most important. Most people don't argue with someone who values respect so fiercely that he's going to carry out every threat he makes. Above all, *never* make a threat you're simply not prepared to carry out. Bluffing threats are for amateurs. Sooner or later you're going to be called. When that happens, you'd better do what you said or leave town. You can send the two grand to the publishers.

3

Kidnapping

LITTLE JOHNNY TAKES A RIDE

They picked him up on his way home from school. Poor little Johnny, bundled into a car by two strange men and driven off into the night, sobbing on the phone as he told you he was all right. Faint but pathetic screams as they gave him a taste of what would happen if you didn't come up with your last quarter million in unmarked bills. Or if you called the cops.

This time they got it right. Last time someone called at two o'clock in the morning they were threatening to kill your wife, the same wife you were frantically trying to divorce. She was asking more in alimony than those jokers wanted for a ransom. That time saying no was the cheap solution. But you've grown kind of fond of little Johnny over the past ten years.

Of course, they may kill him anyway. In this city a person can serve almost as much time for kidnapping as for murder. What have they got to lose by throwing him out of a plane circulating 10,000 feet over your back garden? If they've got the money anyway, why hand back a ten-year-old sack full of evidence, alive and talking? If they haven't got the money, Johnny is the key witness who may well put them behind bars.

They said they would call back in four hours. That's when they give you the details of where to leave the money and so forth. It had better be a foolproof system. You're not going to part with one red cent until you see the whites of Johnny's eyes. Meanwhile you've got four hours to decide what to do. Call the cops? Sit on your hands? Wake up the bank manager?

First, you have to consider how you feel about what might happen. Most of all, you would like not to pay and still get little Johnny back in one piece. The worst that can happen is to have him killed when you've paid anyway. Between these two options you prefer paying and having him safe to not paying and having him killed. That's where they made their mistake with your late wife. As far as little Johnny is concerned, you feel like this:

		Kidnapper	
		No kill	Kill
	Pay	2nd	4th
You	No pay	1st	3rd

How you feel about the world the night little Johnny takes a ride

This puts you in the same position as the freelance extortion victim, provided that the kidnapper is smart enough to snatch someone you're prepared to pay for, and provided that the demand is not too greedy. If they'd kidnapped your canary and demanded your worldly wealth, you'd have told them to kiss off. If you'd taught your canary to do amusing tricks and squeal blood-curdling oaths at your enemies, you might have paid a hundred or two for its safe return. But they kidnapped your only begotten son, and you'd part with all you have to see him safe at home again. Next you must decide how the kidnappers feel about things. To do this, you need to decide whether they're freelance or professional operators.

Freelance kidnapping

Assume for the moment that they're freelances. If they get the money, would they rather kill little Johnny or hand him back? There are two schools of thought on this matter. One kidnapper will expect all of the aggravation and inconvenience caused by killing the hostage to outweigh by far any minor benefit arising from eliminating a key witness. The legal establishment takes a dim view of kidnapping, whether it is successful or abortive. Despite this, it does not stir up the same heat for kidnapping as for outright murder. There is therefore less chance of being caught for kidnapping than for murder, while penalties for the unlucky ones will be a little less severe. Another kidnapper will think differently, reckoning that kidnapping brings *nearly* as much heat, penalties *nearly* as heavy, as murder. Maybe killing the hostage and getting rid of all that evidence cuts down the risk of capture and conviction so markedly that it's the most sensible thing to do. The first type of kidnapper, a Nice Freelance, thinks like this about the world:

		Nice Freelance	
		No kill	Kill
You	Pay	1st	2nd
	No pay	3rd	4th

Nice Freelance kidnapper's preferences concerning the fate of young John

From this we can see that the Nice Freelance is no softie. He plans a snatch, knowing that it may well be necessary to kill the hostage. Nevertheless, the best thing that can happen to him is to get the money without having to kill the hostage — pay/no kill. This produces all the profit and less heat. The worst that can happen is to get no money and kill the hostage — no pay/kill (all heat and no money). Being something of a desperado, the Nice Freelance would rather kill and get the money than not kill and go broke. He wants above all to be paid but, as a matter of fact, has a dominant strategy that is not to kill the hostage. He would prefer to spare little Johnny if he gets paid, and he would prefer to spare him if he doesn't get paid. If Johnny has taken a ride with a Nice Freelance, your problem looks like this:

Nice Freelance

		No kill	Kill
You	Pay	1st 2nd	2nd 4th
	No pay	3rd 1st	4th 3rd

You vs. the Nice Freelance in the case of lucky LJ's brief captivity

Both of you have dominant strategies. You would rather not pay if Johnny bites the dust, and you would rather not pay if he doesn't. The Nice Freelance would rather not kill the little chap, whether or not you pay. In this case, the outcome is quite straightforward. It is no pay/no kill, your first choice. Since you both have dominant strategies, no one has any incentive to seize the first move, to force the opposition to move first, or anything else. Since the likely outcome is your first choice, you can hardly be expected to listen to any deal. You just don't pay; you sit tight, and you hope that you guessed right. This, of course, will take some considerable nerve when you flick through Johnny's photos in the family album, but it is without doubt the most sensible thing to do. On the other end of the telephone line the Nice Freelance is coming to the conclusion that kidnapping does not look like a good choice of occupation for people who think like he does. He may strike lucky and always choose stupid victims who can't think things through. More plausibly — and I'll come back to this — he may be able to sow a seed of doubt in the victim's mind about the possibility that he is not Nice at all but in fact as Nasty as can be. Failing this, he should hang up his phone and retire.

The Nasty Freelance, on the other hand, wants to destroy the evidence, whether or not he gets paid:

Nasty Freelance

	No kill	Kill
Pay	2nd	1st
No pay	4th	3rd

The Nasty Freelance's preferences

Killing the hostage is his dominant strategy, preferred whether the victim pays or not. The Nasty Freelance is no psychopath; he prefers to have the money and let the hostage go home if the only alternative is killing the hostage for nothing. The best thing that can happen is getting paid and killing the hostage, leaving no evidence and acquiring all the cash. The worst thing that can happen is no money and a live witness — no pay/no kill. If the voice on the phone belongs to a Nasty Freelance, your problem looks like this:

Nasty Freelance

	No kill	Kill
Pay	2nd / 2nd	1st / 4th
No pay	4th / 1st	3rd / 3rd

A nasty kidnapping game, in which little Johnny gets wasted if you don't pay up

Once more, both sides have dominant strategies, and it might look as if little Johnny is set for the chop. No pay/kill is what happens when both sides play those dominant strategies, and it doesn't make any difference who makes the first move. If you jump in quickly and pay up, you won't save little Johnny's life. The Nasty Freelance wastes him anyway. If you wait for the kidnapper to make the first move, that move is going to be lethal.

But, but, but — your darling son isn't quite dead yet. If both you and the kidnapper can think straight, you'll both realize that playing your dominant strategies produces an outcome that *you both want to avoid*: no pay/kill. If little Johnny had nine lives, you'd really be in business. You could make it clear to the kidnapper that you'll pay *this time*, but *next time* you'll pay only if he has spared Johnny's Number One Life, or you could suggest a deal that offered to pay for Life Two provided that Life One had been spared and so on. It's not worth going into the ins and outs of this deal at the moment, since your young son most assuredly has only one life. If you had a large family and he'd kidnapped them all, you might try and retrieve them one by one in this manner. We'll come back to mass kidnapping later on.

Johnny's life depends on the fact that *both* sides prefer pay/no kill to no pay/kill. You need to do a deal with the kidnapper, yet whoever makes the first move is bound to be double-crossed. If you pay first, the kidnapper tears up the deal and slits Johnny's throat. If he releases Johnny first, you go running back to the bank with your life savings. Each wants his move to be conditional on the move of the other; both want to move second. This is quite tricky a puzzle to solve. Perhaps the money could be chained to a railing at one end of a bridge and little Johnny chained to a railing at the other. You could walk towards the kidnapper, exchange keys as you passed and walk on to unchain your respective prizes. But what if the kidnapper shoots you, takes your keys, kills Johnny and escapes with the money? What if your suitcase is full of torn-up newspaper? You could both come equipped with .357 magnums and insert the barrels into each other's mouths while he counts the cash and you check out LJ for serious damage. Nothing, however, is foolproof. Although we might expect considerable energy to be devoted to devising new ruses for making the switch, every method is bound to give a slight advantage to one side or the other. In practice, of course, nearly all switches give a considerable advantage to the kidnapper, who plays on the fact that the victim is not thinking clearly. Much as you love little Johnny, you must force yourself to keep remembering that his captor has snatched him only to get his hands on your money: as long as you've got the money, you've got bargaining power. Don't sell yourself short. If the kidnapper is Nice, he's not going to slit your son's throat. If he's Nasty, he'd still rather have the money than not.

What is quite clear is that a third party can come to the rescue. If a stakeholder can be found who is trusted by both sides, then the problem is solved. You give the middle-man the money; the kidnapper gives him Johnny. He makes the switch. If he doesn't get both the money and the hostage, the deal is off. The stakeholder, of course, commands a fat fee for his services. A professional stakeholder has his business reputation to consider. He has a strong incentive to be impartial, since impartiality is what he is selling. If such mediation can be found, then there is a deal available that will make every one happy, although once more we have the spectacle of victim forced to collude with criminal, anxious to commit himself to *not* playing his dominant strategy. Kidnapper and victim achieve pay/no kill rather than no pay/kill if they can find a third party to guarantee their deal.

There may be something of a problem over who, precisely, the middle person might be. The kidnapper won't be too pleased by a mediator who is too close to the forces of justice. You won't be too pleased by the Nasty Freelance's best friend. The lawyers won't touch it, and anyway the kidnapper wouldn't stand a chance if he tried to sue you for breach of contract. A professional villain, however, will do nicely. Someone who sets great store by respect is going to stand by her word, because that's why people respect her and keep on going back to do business with her. Any kidnapper or victim who tries to double-cross her is in for a rough ride. You call a friend of yours, who turns out to know someone who knows someone. You get the phone number, and eventually a serious-sounding person with no name agrees to help you out for some 25 per cent of the ransom money. This is a bargain if it makes the deal work, and you agree right away.

When all of this blows over you could set yourself up in business. The legal waters may be a little murky (something about being an accessory to kidnapping), but anyone who brings in a professional will already have decided not to call the cops. All you have to do is float a company called Ultimate Broking and sell impartiality. You take your commission, and you don't preach sermons. You also create a lot of happiness in the process, since each side is simply longing for the deal to work, crying out for someone to help them make it happen.

Failing an intermediary or a foolproof ruse for making the switch, little Johnny is in dire straits. While no one really wants him to die, neither side can trust the other enough to avoid kill/no pay.

Given an intermediary, a Nasty Freelance is much more likely to make money than a Nice One. The difference between them is that, given the relative penalties for kidnap and murder, the Nasty Freelance feels that eliminating the person most likely to put him behind bars more than compensates for the graver penalties if he does get caught. This suggests that hostages' lives might be saved by *reducing* the penalties for kidnap in relation to those for *murder*. Given the fixed benefit of eliminating a hostile witness, a bigger difference between the penalties for kidnap and murder would produce more Nice Freelances. After all, if kidnap and murder result in the same jail sentence, it is worth killing the hostage for almost any reduction in the risk of conviction. A large difference in the sentences, by producing more Nice Freelances, should reduce kidnapping. Nice Freelances would then be almost bound to fail.

All of this is pretty straightforward, if a trifle hard on John Junior (though there really is no point in throwing your money away if he's to be killed anyway). Your big problem, of course, is knowing whether the kidnapper in question is Nice or Nasty. Even Nice ones must sound pretty ferocious over the phone if they hold out any hope of making money. Only the most stupid of Nice Freelances will tell you that they have no intention of killing your missing offspring. Of course, you will never *really* know the contents of a kidnapper's brain. (Inexperienced kidnappers will not even know this themselves.) You have to guess, to take a chance. It may sound a little callous to gamble with the life of a frightened ten-year-old. You probably think that you would never dream of doing such a thing, that Johnny is priceless. Not so. What you mean is that if there was a fifty-fifty chance that the man on the phone was Nasty, you'd pay up at the speed of light. Very commendable. But what if there was a one-in-a-hundred chance? Maybe you'd think twice, but you'd pay up because you're a goody-goody.

Yet you take small chances with the boy's life every day of the year. Every time he walks out of your front door there's a one-in-a-billion chance he'll be struck by lightning. Yet you let him walk on out. Every time you race him to school in your turbo-charged '69 Camaro you shorten his odds considerably. You race him to school once a week. If you picked up the phone one day and heard some squeaky voice demanding a million dollars, with Johnny giggling in the background, you wouldn't burn rubber all the way to the bank. Yet there would still be a tiny chance he was in serious trouble.

What you really mean when you say you wouldn't gamble with his life is that he's a nice little chap and you'd want pretty good odds for him. If he really is gone and that really is him screaming down the phone, however, you'll probably crack and pay up. All I'm saying is, think twice. You'll feel pretty stupid handing over a quarter of a million to some senile Father Christmas with a wooden leg, even if it's just possible he's a Nasty Santa.

Uncertainty is the kidnapper's bread and butter. The occasional Nasty Freelance makes life much sweeter for the Nice ones, who'd otherwise quickly go bankrupt. Even if only one kidnapper in ten would rather kill the hostage, most victims aren't prepared to take the chance. They pay up for the same reason that people take out insurance. They know it's probably a bad deal, but they can't bear the thought of what will happen if things go badly wrong.

If you decide to take a gamble on whether the villain is Nice or Nasty, however, you should consider whether little Johnny could identify his captors if he makes it home alive. If Johnny was your pet canary, the question wouldn't arise. If Johnny was only six months old, he wouldn't make much of a prosecution witness. That would mean the kidnapper would have no real incentive to kill him; it should make you feel better and less inclined to pay up. But Johnny is ten. He could point out the kidnapper in an identification parade — *if* he has seen him, that is.

Sometimes hostages are blindfolded, and there is then obviously a much slimmer chance of identification. This means that if Johnny *is* blindfolded, you should be less inclined to pay up. The chances that the kidnapper has a Nice attitude to him are much greater, since he represents less of a threat. This gives rise to a paradox. It seems to be safer to kidnap a canary or an infant, or to blindfold your hostage if he can incriminate you, but this cuts down the chance of being paid off by a victim who figures the angles. A hard-headed kidnapper who really wants to make a success of things, therefore, should rip the blindfold off as soon as he arrives at the hide-out. He should make sure that the hostage sees him and that the victim knows this. The fact that the hostage can put the kidnapper behind bars means that the kidnapper has a strong incentive to eliminate him. This is a strong bargaining counter. A kidnapper needs the victim to think that he has an incentive to kill the hostage, and the threat of recognition is just such an incentive. Blindfolding hostages may make him feel safe, but all it represents is a safe way of going bankrupt.

Calling the cops

At the end of the day little Johnny is home in bed, safe and sound. He made it because you paid the money. There's a 90 per cent chance he'd be home in bed even if you had refused to pay up. So why didn't you call the cops?

The voice on the phone was pretty emphatic. The kidnapper made Johnny scream a bit while he told you what he'd do if you called the police. You didn't call them because you were scared that the little fellow would get bumped off. A Nice Kidnapper wouldn't do a thing like that, but if you were sure you were dealing with a Nice Kidnapper, you'd have refused to pay anyway. Once you'd taken this decision, you would have had nothing to lose by calling in the cavalry. You paid because you couldn't rule out the chance that the man on the phone was not nice at all. You believed that he'd kill LJ at the first scent of a member of the law enforcement profession.

The police will take a tough line on kidnapping. They want to discourage the others. They don't get any medals for helping distraught parents pay to get their kids home safe and sound. They get promoted for busting villains. That doesn't mean to say that they would rather see Johnny dead than alive. They want to save his life, but they also have to think of all the other kidnappers who will be encouraged if kidnapping looks like an easy way to make money. As a victim, you are going to be much more prepared to pay than they are:

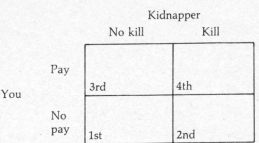

Police preferences in the kidnap game

The cops want to fix things so that the kidnapper gets caught. This means that they can help only when you have decided not to pay. At that stage you might as well call them on the off chance that you've made a mistake and decided not to pay someone who's going to kill little Johnny. They might just get him out alive. But if you know who you're dealing with, you steer well clear of the forces of justice. If you're dealing with a Nice Freelance, you're not going to pay, and the kidnapper is going to let Johnny go. No role for the police there. If you're dealing with a Nasty one, you're going to pay, and the cops will only get in the way.

The Nasty Freelance, provided that he can get his message across, forces the victim to protect him from the police. Both he and the victim prefer pay/no kill to no pay/kill and both collude to exclude the cops so that they can achieve a deal. Even when the cops call you and ask if everything is OK, you're going to tell them lies to protect the man who has threatened to kill your son. That's why we don't hear too much about successful kidnappings. It's not because they haven't happened; it's because nobody wants you to find out about them.

Professional kidnapping

Unlike extortion, kidnapping offers some scope for a determined villain, who gets paid if the victim believes that he's really prepared to kill the hostage. Compared with protection, the big disadvantage of kidnapping is the nuisance and expense of snatching some snivelling kid, feeding him, phoning his parents and making the switch without getting caught. Worse, there is always the risk of being forced to kill the hostage and then being hunted for murder.

The big payoffs that can be earned by kidnappers can be made more secure if they build a solid reputation. A professional kidnapper does not work towards a single huge payoff but looks for a long succession of huge payoffs. Each depends on those that have gone before, because the professional keeps his word and can be trusted by the victim.

The professional kidnapper offers the same deal as the freelance, pay/no kill or no pay/kill.

Once offered, however, the deal must be honoured above all else. Pay/no kill and no pay/kill are the top two choices, with pay/no kill as the best possible outcome. If the deal falls through, it is obviously better to have the money (pay/kill) than not (no pay/no kill). Not getting paid *and* not carrying out the death threat is the worst thing that can happen, representing the first step on the road to ruin:

	Pro kidnapper	
	No kill	Kill
Victim — Pay	1st	3rd
Victim — No pay	4th	2nd

Professional kidnapper's preferences

When you're set up as a fully professional kidnapper with a solid reputation for straight dealing, you can't lose if you stick to freelance victims:

	Pro kidnapper	
	No kill	Kill
Pay	1st / 2nd	3rd / 4th
No pay	4th / 1st	2nd / 3rd

Victim (freelance)

Professional kidnapper and freelance victim: the stakes

The freelance victim is the same freelance as before and still has a dominant strategy. This is still not paying. The pro kidnapper does not have a clear-cut choice. This is his great strength. He would rather kill if the victim doesn't pay, and he would rather not kill if the victim pays. This means that the order in which the players make their moves is now critical. A deadline will therefore be needed to enable everyone to decide when the victim has actively *not paid* and when he has simply not got around to paying *yet*. The deadline enables the kidnapper to force the first move upon the victim but, in this case, is not strictly necessary. Most freelance victims who find themselves up against a pro will be rushing to make the first move — and that first move will be paying. This is because if the victim left the first move to the kidnapper, there would be no alternative to his killing the hostage. If the hostage was allowed to live, the victim obviously wouldn't pay, and this would produce the worst possible outcome for a pro kidnapper. Forced to move first, the kidnapper must kill, and the outcome is kill/no pay, which both sides want to avoid. So the victim won't try to force the kidnapper into a hasty move and has no choice but to pay up quickly. The outcome is pay/no kill, the best possible payoff for the pro kidnapper and also the one preferred by the victim to the only other feasible alternative, which is no pay/kill. The victim is forced to collude with the kidnapper.

Provided that neither side is in any doubt that the kidnapper is indeed a pro, the undertaking seems to involve little risk. A very important aspect of the business, therefore, is the development of a distinctive trade mark. That way the two-bit hucksters in the city can't cling to the coat tails of a successful professional operator. A black hand on the ransom note has, of course, already been patented, but a little ingenuity should enable anyone to come up with a mark that gives their kidnappings an unmistakable air of authenticity. Once you have established this mark, the services of a reputable competition-regulation agency (see chapter 5) will — in exchange for a slice of the action — protect it against imposters.

With a tough reputation, it should hardly ever be

necessary to kill hostages. This has the great advantage that the heat will rarely get too serious. Compare a professional kidnapping with an armed robbery, which usually generates enormous police activity, whatever the payoff. Kidnapping should be a much safer way of making the same kind of cash. The risks can be further reduced by threatening to kill the hostage at any time in the future if the victim ever calls the cops. Having got to the hostage once, it is always plausible you can hit him again, though if the threat is called, it must be carried out. If you can get away with threats like this, the police will hardly ever be involved. Your only problem then will be that kidnapping might seem too much like any other nine-to-five job.

Professional victims

For most victims every kidnap is a one-off disaster. Most will be bankrupt by the time it is all over, so the possibility of future attempts can be discounted. Most private individuals have limited means and therefore represent a restricted market for repeated kidnappings. They certainly can't come up with the sort of money available to a large multinational company or even a government. Big companies have in the past paid up to $50 million to retrieve senior executives from the clutches of unscrupulous desperados. That grey little man in the pin-striped suit can quickly become the most lovable chap in the whole world once he is tied up and hauled off to some Central American jungle. It is often difficult to see why his hard-nosed colleagues pay up. You would think that, trained as they are to ride roughshod over the competition at all costs, they would have more sense. But they *do* pay, so there's money to be made. This is despite the fact that, at first sight, things don't look too hopeful. The stakes, of course, are higher all round. Companies have come to expect their executives to be kidnapped once in a while and are apt to equip them with bullet-proof cars, guns, bodyguards and other hardware designed to make the snatch more difficult. More important, they expect more kidnappings in the future. They too have reputations to consider. Pro victims, be they multinational corporations or governments, know that if they give in this time, they may be forced to give in again the next. Taking this long-term view, they'd rather not pay (seeing the hostage killed but preserving their own reputation) than pay and save his life. They can justify this attitude to themselves and anyone else who might be interested by claiming that it not only saves them money but also saves lives in the long term. A tough line now means fewer future hostages. The hard-nosed pro victim therefore thinks like this:

Kidnapper

	No kill	Kill
Pro victim — Pay	3rd	4th
Pro victim — No pay	1st	2nd

Pro victim's preferences in the kidnap game

When a pro victim meets a Nice Freelance, the result is a foregone conclusion:

Nice Freelance

	No kill	Kill
Pro victim — Pay	3rd / 1st	4th / 2nd
Pro victim — No pay	1st / 3rd	2nd / 4th

A pro victim destroys a Nice Freelance kidnapper

The Nice Freelance hasn't got a prayer. Both sides have dominant strategies. The result of these, no pay/no kill, is the victim's first choice, so it is likely to be pretty stable. The order of moves doesn't make any difference, and the victim has no incentive to deal. This sort of kidnapping is a waste of time, and we begin to see why the Nice Freelance Kidnapper seems such a contradiction in terms. While Nice Kidnappers are both a theoretical and a practical possibility, the payoff matrices show them to be a doomed species. Once upon a time, they may well have existed, but the process of natural selection weeded them out long ago.

The Nasty Freelance is not much better off when faced by a pro:

Nasty Freelance

		No kill	Kill
		2nd	1st
	Pay		
		3rd	4th
Pro victim			
	No	4th	3rd
	pay		
		1st	2nd

The Nasty Freelance meets his match in a hard-hearted pro victim

The Nasty Freelance and the pro victim have such dramatically opposed views about the world that they have nothing to talk to each other about. As a matter of fact, we have here an example of a game of pure conflict. From this we can see that the confrontation between a Nasty Freelance and a pro victim is no different, in any significant way, from a bank robbery. No dealing, no talking and, since both have dominant strategies, the order of moves makes no difference. No pay/kill looks inevitable. This is not much fun for the kidnapper, who is no psychopath. Nasty Freelances should concentrate on freelance victims, who pay up and keep quiet. While the pro kidnapper has no dominant strategy, there's no advantage in making the victim move first. The victim won't pay whenever he moves, since paying guarantees one or other of the two worst things which can happen to him. A hard-nosed pro will simply let the hostage die in order to protect his reputation for tough dealing, but won't get into this position in the first place if he can see it coming.

The all-pro game seems just as simple:

Pro kidnapper

		No kill	Kill

All-pro kidnap confrontation

Who, then, makes money out of professional victims? Someone must, since international companies have paid out huge sums over the years. In part this is because some pros have soft noses. Companies grow attached to their executives. Having grown attached, they don't think clearly in a crisis. Protecting your reputation is fine in theory, but when friendly old Joe Smith is hauled off and locked up in a dirty cellar, when his wife and kids are weeping at home, things look different. The company is liable to forget it's a pro victim and pay up like a freelance.

The chance to save the life of a genuine walking, talking person is a high-speed nose-softener. After all, everyone knows that hundreds of lives could be saved every year on the roads by dropping the speed limit by ten miles an hour. Knowing this, most of us sentence those hundreds to death by refusing to do this, just so that we can enjoy the trivial pleasure of driving a little faster. We might feel a little differently about the speed limit if we were invited to meet next year's victims. If the government sponsored a television documentary giving intimate details of the everyday lives, the hopes and fears, of the very people who will die next year if the speed limit is not lowered, we might even vote to lower it. The arithmetic is identical, but we just don't react the same way.

A company that protects its hard reputation for not paying is saving potential future kidnap victims' lives. Yet when it comes to the crunch, old Joe's tear-stained kids may make it easier to sentence twenty anonymous executives to death in the future in exchange for saving one life today. In this respect, kidnapping is not quite like protection. There is no guarantee that a professional victim will behave professionally when the chips are down.

Another thing that is going to increase the incentive to pay is kidnap insurance. Lloyds of London, for example, has been writing kidnap policies for years, while Dutch shipowners formed mutual insurance societies as far back as the eighteenth century to cover the cost of ransoms demanded by pirates who kidnapped their crews in the East Indies. The insurance itself, of course, is unremarkable. After all, anyone can insure himself against theft, and few would argue that this increases the number of thefts. What is much more unusual is the fact that the insurers usually insist that kidnap negotiations are handled by them or their nominees. The insurance company ends up colluding with the criminal to pay the ransom. The legal position here is confused, although kidnap insurance does not in itself make life much easier for kidnappers.

The kidnap policy is usually top secret and void if its existence is admitted by the company insured. This makes evidence on the scale of kidnap insurance difficult to collect. The reason for the secrecy is, presumably, that the insurers fear that kidnap attempts against their clients will be more likely if it is known that the victims will not be spending their own cash if they give in. It is thus hard to reconcile the insurers' protests that kidnap insurance does not encourage the crime with their simultaneous insistence that specific policies be kept secret. Be that as it may, there's no doubt that, if you are fortunate enough to hit someone who is insured against kidnap, life will be a lot easier. He won't care so much about the money, or even about his reputation, unless there's a chance that the insurance will be withdrawn. This should make an otherwise professional victim think like a freelance, and this in itself increases the chances of getting paid.

Remember that when the freelance victim meets the Nasty Kidnapper, there is an opening for a middle-man. Sure enough, when you hit someone insured by Lloyds, an organization called Control Risks will probably come into the picture. Control Risks is a private company, formed in 1975, that 'advises' in kidnap negotiations and helps Lloyds to assess risks. No one announces the presence of kidnap insurance loss adjusters, since kidnappers would raise their demands sky-high, but Lloyds and Control Risks pride themselves on the high proportion of hostages whom they have extracted alive. Indeed, any company that takes out kidnap insurance with Lloyds agrees to allow Control Risks to handle the negotiations. This means that you're almost bound to make money when they're involved. They may beat you down a bit, but you should always raise an opening bid against a corporate victim in anticipation of this.

The other nose-softening technique that may shake a ransom out of a professional victim is a promise of total secrecy. People who are concerned with their reputation don't want to back down *in public*. This is what lays them open to defeat in the future. If the kidnapper can guarantee a professional victim that he won't have to back down *publicly*, the victim loses no respect in the eyes of other potential opponents. This way, a pro victim may once more start to think like a freelance. It means that the hostage you capture shouldn't be too famous, since once a hostage is publicly missed, secrecy is not a possibility.

As it happens, the offer of secrecy is more plausible if it is made by a freelance kidnapper. Once the deal is consummated, the freelance has no incentive to reveal his existence. Indeed, he has every incentive to keep it quiet, since publicity increases his chances of getting caught. The professional kidnapper, on the other hand, may promise secrecy but is less credible. The professional lives on his reputation, and secret deals do nothing to enhance this.

If a freelance can snatch a hostage secretly, a pro victim may be tempted to believe an offer of continued silence. When this happens, the pro victim decides to pay, for the reasons we discussed above. Paying will be made much easier by the existence of a discreet professional intermediary. This begins to look like a near-perfect business venture, the existence of which neither victim nor kidnapper has any incentive to reveal. An ordinary freelance victim may well pay you but has no reason to keep the kidnapping a secret. An ordinary pro victim won't pay. A pro victim facing a Nasty Freelance kidnapper who has made an offer of secrecy has all the incentives of a freelance victim to pay, combined with the desire of a professional to keep quiet. For obvious reasons, this scenario also offers the most lucrative openings for the professional intermediary.

Anyone who is thinking of trying the Secret Snatch won't have much hard evidence to draw inspiration from. Such evidence, by definition, will be almost impossible to obtain. The set-up is so nearly foolproof, however, that it must have succeeded many times. Professional victims, such as large companies, must from time to time be faced with successful secret freelance kidnappings that are negotiated by secret professional intermediaries.

THE DUNNE KIDNAP

The story

On Friday, 16 October 1981, Ben Dunne Junior was driving his father's black Mercedes from Dublin to Newry. Reputed to be one of the richest men in Ireland, Ben Junior was a leading light in his family's chain store business, which owns sixty-six shops and an annual turnover in the region of £200 million. Ben Dunne Senior, who over forty years had built the business from nothing, had been planning to accompany his son on the trip to open a new outlet in Portadown. At the last minute he changed his mind and Ben Junior went on alone.

He had just crossed the border into Northern Ireland.

Under the noses of a British SAS observation post two hundred yards away in Killeen, four armed and masked men somehow managed to get Dunne's Mercedes to stop. One account has it that a green Opel Ascona swerved in front of Dunne's car, that Dunne avoided a crash, drove on for a hundred yards or so, pulled up and walked back to argue with the driver of the Opel. This would appear to be a remarkable way to plan a kidnap, but, whatever happened, Dunne was bundled into the green Ascona. They raced back across the border into the Republic, drove for about thirty minutes, and ended up outside a shed somewhere back in the North. Dunne says that immediately after this he was asked for the telephone numbers of his father and of Mary, his wife. He was then forced to lie down, with Armalite rifles pressed into his neck and chest.

After a while, the group set off on a long cross-country trek over fields and ditches, holding Ben Dunne for a time in a ditch before driving him to a nearby house. Here he remained with his captors for six days. According to Dunne, he was forced to lie down for most of the time, and 'it was made very clear that I would be shot if I lifted my head and saw anything.' Elsewhere, the plot thickened.

At this stage, security forces on both sides of the border had no idea where Dunne was being held. What was described as a 'full-scale search operation' was launched by the Gardai to the south, and the Royal Ulster Constabulary (RUC) and the British Army to the north, of the border. South Armagh is an area in which the security forces have been unable to operate normally for a number of years. Thus the British Army used its normal method of combining random road blocks with helicopter drops of small patrols of soldiers. The Army does not engaged in extensive foot patrols in bandit country. RUC patrols venture with considerable circumspection outside fortresses at Crossmaglen and Forkhill.

The ransom was fixed at £500,000 in cash, and the first attempt to pay was made the following day, Saturday, 17 October. An intermediary drove from Dublin to Dundalk in a car loaded either with the full half-million or with £300,000, depending on whom you believe. As he was making for a rendezvous just outside the town, he was intercepted by the Gardai. The man and his money were sent back to Dublin. The Dunne family immediately issued a statement claiming that they had nothing to do with the thwarting of the attempted payoff. Mary Dunne claimed that the family had 'made every attempt to fulfil the request of Bernard's abducters' and that they were prepared to try again to pay the money. At least one member of the family was staying at the Fairways Hotel, Dundalk, waiting to be contacted.

Meanwhile, statements began to proliferate. The Provisional IRA in Dublin issued a statement denying any involvement in the affair. Given the fact that the Provos had not previously kidnapped for money and were not thought to be short of ready cash, this statement was generally accepted. Suspicion settled on the Irish National Liberation Army (INLA), which did have cash-flow problems. As far as could be seen, no political demands had been made, and the cash was the only condition for Dunne's release. Cardinal Thomas O'Fiach, leader of the Catholic Church in Ireland, issued a statement supporting Irish government intervention, on the grounds that to pay this time would only encourage other attempts.

The following day, Father Dermot McCarthy, a 'family friend', was interrupted during a meeting with certain people at a derelict house in Skyhill. Father McCarthy had been told to go to a rendezvous, where he was met by two masked men with Armalite rifles. He drove his car close to the house and was met by another masked man, who told him that Dunne was still alive and was worried about his wife and family. Shortly afterwards, police arrived on the scene, and there was a brief but brisk exchange of fire. A number of armed men retreated to safety north of the border. Father McCarthy was arrested and then released.

Next day, Monday, a large cash sum for the ransom was once more intercepted by the police, amid much publicity. This time, on the basis of a tip-off from the Gardai, the RUC stopped two cars carrying the cash north of the border. Once more, the intermediaries were quickly sent back to where they had come from. By now, an enormous phone-tapping operation was being undertaken in Dublin. This aimed at covering all lines related to the Dunne family and included phones at Blackrock, Castleknock, Dun Laoghaire, Portmarnock and Malahide. A computerized fifty-line scanner was used to monitor all lines into the Dunnes' Dublin business headquarters. In addition, the Gardai claimed to have detectives in every branch of Dunne's stores. Their job was to monitor the cash flowing in and to check that it was all correctly paid into the frozen Dunne bank accounts. Given such an enormous cash turnover, ransom money could easily have been skimmed from a couple of days' takings. There was a lively public debate concerning the morality of the apparent determination of the Dublin government to prevent the family from securing Ben Dunne's release by paying the ransom.

North of the border, the RUC took similar steps, which amounted to seizing temporary control of the Dunne company's cash and were of untested legality. Mary Dunne responded with the statement 'I will do whatever the kidnappers want to get my husband back. His release is my only priority.' The two vehicles used in the kidnap were found in flames just north of the border.

During the course of Wednesday Father McCarthy, the family friend, made an emotional broadcast appeal to the kidnappers. He urged them to cut their losses and to release Dunne, since the security forces were closing in and nothing could be gained by continuing. By all accounts, the broadcast had considerable national impact.

Some time late on Wednesday night, Eamon Mallie, a locally born but Belfast-based journalist with Downtown Radio received a phone call at his parents' home near Crossmaglen. The call was obviously made locally, and someone with a local accent told him that 'the man who is missing can be picked up at Cullyhanna Parochial House.'

This was about five miles from Mallie, and Mallie set off at 11 p.m. He arrived to find a dishevelled figure wandering around. This turned out to be Dunne, who had been waiting outside for thirty minutes, despite the fact that the lights in the Parochial House were clearly visible. *At 12.15,* Mallie and Dunne rang the doorbell.

The local priest was Father O'Neill. He let the journalist and the kidnap victim use his phone, and several calls were made. None of these was to the Dunne family, although one was to a family friend in the Dublin area. They left Father O'Neill's house at about one o'clock in the morning, driving back across the border into the Republic on the Dundalk — Newtonhamilton road. This is an approved crossing, yet no police check points were encountered. Their car was stopped by the Gardai some time later, but only Mallie was asked to identify himself. Dunne's wife was finally contacted from a coinbox phone at about 2.30 a.m. This was the first news the family had of the release. At no stage before Dunne returned home were the Gardai contacted, although some stories have it that all road blocks were lifted, without explanation, at 3 a.m.

Both the family and the police continue to insist that no ransom was paid.

The loose ends and the theories

Precisely what happened will no doubt never be publicly revealed. It is possible, however, to make a number of plausible assumptions, to isolate some loose ends, and to attempt to reconcile these with the range of theories that circulated after the event. First, the loose ends.

The kidnapping itself seems to have been a rather haphazard affair. While it is not quite clear how the kidnappers forced Dunne to stop, his car was not seriously damaged. They must anyway either have had extremely good information about his movements and route or taken a considerable chance hanging around waiting for him to show up. Most kidnappings occur within a few hundred yards of either the hostage's home or his place of work. On the other hand, Dunne was taken on the main Dublin—Belfast road. It was predictable that he would have crossed at this point, and an alternative legal route would have involved a considerable detour. If the four kidnappers tried and failed to ram Dunne's Mercedes with their green Ascona, they must have been delighted when he stopped and walked back towards them.

The point at which this road meets the border is close to the safe havens of South Armagh. This has a bearing on one element shared by most of the theories, which is that the kidnap gang comprised a mixture of breakaway Provos from South Armagh and some independent gangsters. It is widely believed that the kidnapping was a contract job on behalf of the INLA. The Armalite rifles used (and three Armalite cartridges were given to Dunne as a souvenir of his release) are Provo favourites, and the Dublin Provisionals clearly believed that some of its ex-members were involved. Little love is lost between the Provos and the INLA. The location of the kidnap lends some support to this theory. Quite apart from the fact that the Provisionals had not previously kidnapped for money, they are presumably sufficiently well organized to have pulled off a safer and more conventional snatch, which could have taken place close to Dunne's home or to his destination. They did not need to run the risks associated with waiting around by a main road and hoping that they would be able to get Dunne's car to stop. On the other hand, a breakaway group from South Armagh, operating in the face of the severe disapproval of Dublin command, could not have done anything else. It is highly unlikely that it would have been able to kidnap and hold Dunne in the Republic, or to have got him across the border, with both the security forces and the Provos looking for it. While the limited number of approved crossings makes a snatch near the border a reasonable bet, taking the hostage so far from either home or destination is a highly untypical feature of kidnapping and, for an organized professional, unnecessary.

The second loose end concerns the ransom money and the intermediaries' frequent encounters with the police. There is no legal offence of kidnapping in the Irish Republic; instead there exists the crime of 'unlawful imprisonment'. Thus the payment of a kidnap ransom has no special place in law, and the intermediaries were prima facie accessories to a serious crime. The ransom money was crucial material evidence. Despite this, the intermediaries appear hardly to have been questioned, much less arrested, by either the RUC or the Gardai. The money was never held, despite the elaborate process of putting detectives into every Dunne's store to prohibit the skimming of used notes for ransom payment. This was possibly because the intervention of the police in this way, just like the taking control of Dunne's cash flow, was of untested legality. It is certainly a loose end, however.

The third loose end concerns Dunne's release. It was certainly fortunate that Mallie was at his parents' house, so close to the action, at the right time. (Speculation that, as a non-drinker, he would have been the only sober journalist available at such an hour on a Friday night is largely discounted.) One and a quarter hours is a long time to spend driving five miles, meeting Dunne and ringing a doorbell. It is not at all clear why Dunne, on release, waited to be picked up by someone rather than going to the obviously occupied house of the local priest, outside which he had been standing for thirty minutes. It is not clear to whom the phone calls were made after Mallie and Dunne eventually contacted the priest. It *is* clear that they were not to the police and not to Dunne's family; the release was revealed to neither until both men were south of the border. This is consistent with the interpretation that they were concerned not to have immediate dealings with either the British Army or the RUC.

The fourth loose end is the charmed drive back to Dublin, through the thick of an intensive police search on both sides of the border. This may, of course, have been luck.

Turning to the pressures that we can assume motivated the various actors in this drama, the first concerns the Dunnes' perceptions of precisely who the kidnappers were. It seems reasonable to assume that, whoever they were, they would have been people who were concerned with their credibility.

The prospect that the kidnappers would behave like professionals and would carry out their threat if their demands were not met must have been very real. They do not seem to have had an awful lot to lose by killing their hostage, other than the chance of making money. For the Dunnes, the option of outright rejection of the demands, in the hope that the kidnappers would cave in, would clearly have put Ben Dunne's life at risk. Notwithstanding their great wealth and the consequent possibility of a repeat performance, the Dunnes seem to have treated the kidnapping as a one-off problem. Victims who think like this, facing kidnappers with an incentive to kill, will want to pay up, as we have seen. This is consistent with the Dunnes' public stance, which was that of willing victims who were being foiled by the police in their honest attempts to come to terms.

A further pressure bears on a wealthy victim who has decided to pay this time but fears future kidnap attempts. There is a strong incentive to keep the payoff secret. The Irish legal position further complicates this problem. Since there is no crime of kidnapping, anyone involved in paying the ransom, including the family, would be technically guilty of being an accessory to unlawful imprisonment. (This, presumably is the legal basis of police intervention.) A defence of acting under duress would be possible, but things *could* get messy. Much easier to pay in secret.

If the victim has decided not to pay, however, and if it is feared that the kidnappers may kill, he has nothing to lose by appearing to co-operate. Better still, it would clearly be worthwhile for him to appear to be trying to pay but to be thwarted each time by forces beyond his control. This would reduce the chance that the kidnappers might try to bring additional pressure to bear on him by enforcing a deadline, hurting the hostage or whatever. In these circumstances, the victim would have a strong incentive to co-operate with the police. Any kidnap victim who has decided not to pay has this incentive.

Turning to the police, their desire to defeat kidnappers would be consistent with an attempt to thwart a payoff if they feared that this might take place. Under Irish law they could also argue for the legality of this. If the victim has decided to pay up, heavy surveillance of him and intervention in all negotiations would be quite appropriate. If the victim has decided not to pay, the police will presumably want to try to save the hostage's life. They can attempt this by co-operating with the victim in some form of charade. The trouble is, the police will never know for certain what the victim intends to do. Assuming a resourceful victim, it is hard to believe that the police could thwart *every* attempt to make a payoff, particularly if they had no idea who the kidnappers were or where the hostage was being held. (In this example, the problem is further complicated by the border and by the fact that police forces are able not to *control* but merely to *influence* what happens outside their jurisdiction.)

As far as the kidnappers are concerned, there is no reason to suppose that credit would not be claimed for a successful kidnap. The Provisionals have a long history of taking responsibility for events that have provoked a considerably more hostile reaction than this one. It is reasonable to assume that they would have claimed the kidnap if they had been involved. The absence of any claim lends support to the 'freelance kidnap on contract' interpretation. If this is true, the kidnappers themselves had no incentive to claim responsibility, and whoever issued the contract would not have wanted to admit his inability to do the job himself.

How far are these loose ends and assumptions consistent with the various conflicting theories of what really happened? The 'official' version is that the Dunne family really wanted to pay, that the police really wanted them not to. The various police interventions were genuine; the ransom was not paid. Dunne was released as a result partly of Father McCarthy's broadcast appeal and partly of pressure from the Dublin Provisionals, who were fed up with all of the heat generated in one of their traditional stamping grounds. After his release, Ben Dunne bore no grudge against the police for putting his life at risk.

To set against this theory there are three loose ends and

one assumption. If the police and the Dunnes were really at loggerheads, why wasn't the ransom seized and the intermediaries held or at least interrogated? If the ransom wasn't paid, to whom were the phone calls made on Dunne's release, and why did he not let the police and his family know at once? If the police weren't in on the act and didn't know that Dunne had been released, was the charmed drive back to Dublin just luck? If a self-made multi-millionaire, who had built up a chain of sixty-six large stores from nothing, wanted to pay a ransom that he actually had available in cash, would he not have found a way of giving the police the slip or at least of arranging for one of his many business contacts to make the payoff? In favour of the official version is the fact that no one claimed the kidnap (which is a more likely outcome when kidnaps are successful) and the fact that the police did engage in the massive phone-tap operation, which was *not* publicized at the time.

The first of the unofficial theories asserts that the police and the Dunnes were in cahoots. Neither ever intended to pay the ransom, and the widely publicized interventions were an elaborate charade designed both to demoralize the kidnappers and to protect Dunne. The ransom was *not* paid, for the same reasons as those of the official version.

To set against this there is a loose end and an assumption. If the police and the Dunnes were co-operating, why didn't Dunne let his family know as soon as he was released — and who *were* those phone calls to? If the police believed that the Dunnes had decided not to pay, why the elaborate secret phone tap? However, this theory *can* account for the failure to seize the ransom or the intermediaries and the charmed drive back to Dublin (assuming the family friend told the police).

The second conspiracy theory is that the ransom was paid. The theory is identical with the official version, except that it hypothesizes that the Dunnes succeeded in outsmarting the police. It beats the official version by tying up the loose end of the phone calls on release. These would have concerned the details of the exchange. It also seems more plausible to assume that a rich and successful family could find a way to pay if it had really made up its mind to do so. This theory does not tie up the loose ends of the police failure to impound the ransom or the charmed drive back to Dublin, however.

A third theory ties up all the loose ends and every assumption bar one (though this does not mean that it is right). This asserts that *both* unofficial theories are correct at the same time. The Dunnes and the police did co-operate, though neither much trusted the other. The interventions were a charade (hence no seizure). The Dunnes really intended to pay all along, while going along with police advice not to. Since the police suspected the Dunnes, they tapped their phones. The Dunnes succeeded in paying the ransom without the police realizing it (hence the phone calls). The police assumed that the planned co-operation had paid off (hence the charmed drive). The only outstanding problem is why no one claimed a success.

This can be explained two ways. It is possible that the ransom was not paid but promised after the heat had died down and police scrutiny of Dunne assets had relaxed. This is not normally a plausible outcome but, given the long arm of the Irish paramilitaries, is not unrealistic. They could probably have enforced such a contract. The phone calls now become difficult to explain, since they would not have been needed. The other possibility has already been mentioned. If the kidnap was a contract job by freelances, there would have been no incentive to claim responsibility for it.

A final conspiracy theory is a variation on the third. This argues that the Dunnes and the Gardai co-operated, although mistrustfully. The Gardai agreed to the Dunnes' paying the ransom, *provided that this offence was committed north of the border*. This accounts for the phone calls and the charmed drive quite splendidly and for the failure of all concerned to publicize the release until Dunne was well south of the border. If the freelance contract job assumption is correct, no loose ends remain.

Someone with a lot of money knows the truth.

MASS KIDNAPPING: THE IRANIAN HOSTAGES

So far we have discussed kidnapping on a small scale. Taking hostages one at a time is convenient, in the sense that it involves less effort, but it has serious drawbacks in terms of bargaining strategy. With a single hostage, the threat to kill is all or nothing. You can't kill the hostage a little bit. Single hostages are *relatively* indivisible. A desperate kidnapper can engage in limited subdivision but is much more restricted than a colleague with a whole roomful of hostages. A cluster of hostages creates a much stronger bargaining position. It allows for a bigger ransom demand, of course, but that's not the point. Ten hostages won't bring in ten times as much cash as one. The most important point is that they provide the kidnapper with a much better chance of getting paid *at all*. The crucial difference is that they can be released, or killed, one by one. This allows for the use of conditional, tit-for-tat responses by both victim and kidnapper and changes the whole nature of the interaction.

When a group of enthusiastic Iranian students sealed off the US Embassy in Teheran, they bagged two or three rooms full of hostages. They also took on the most experienced professional victim of them all and opened up new vistas for the kidnapping profession. Unlike the normal hijack or siege, the kidnappers were not surrounded. This means that the operation was very like a true kidnap. Even though the victim knew precisely where the hostages were, he could not get at them. Since this was the most public kidnap ever, and since the US government is such a perennial victim, its reputation as a pro victim was absolutely on the line. A secret deal was not possible. Everyone would have noticed.

A tough no-pay policy looked like the obvious answer, yet saturation coverage in the world media quickly established identities for the hostages. Nightly film of weeping relatives made it almost impossible for President Carter to let the hostages die. His last chance to do this evaporated a few hours after the seizure of the Embassy, as the hostages began to develop personalities. However much he might have been prepared to sacrifice the hostages to enhance the US's bargaining reputation, this option was quickly closed off.

There can be no doubt that Carter would dearly have loved to return the Shah if this could have been done without losing face. However, the US had been losing a lot of face since her withdrawal from Vietnam, and he judged that she could not afford to back down again. Furthermore, with his re-election looming and his domestic popularity in decline, he needed a *coup* that might restore his position. Above all, he could not be seen to display any sign of weakness. Carter was therefore wedged firmly between a rock and a hard place.

Back in Iran, the students were probably not *that* keen on killing the hostages. They were, however, very keen indeed on getting the Shah back home. To the extent to which Khomeini was in control of the students, he too had a lot of face to lose. If anything, he was in a tighter bind than Carter. His position in the country depended much more immediately on a high level of popular support. This had been built on taking a tough line with Western 'great powers' but could easily be lost.

Before the saturation coverage by the media, US preferences would probably have produced a game like this:

Iranian students

		No kill	Kill
US government	Pay	1st 3rd	2nd 4th
	No pay	4th 1st	3rd 2nd

US hostages in Iran: Phase One

The crucial element in this interaction is that the US prefers no pay/kill to pay/no kill. This is because she is a professional victim who has lost credibility in recent years. The US has a strongly dominant strategy: no pay. The

Iranian students have no dominant strategy (they prefer to kill if the US doesn't pay, and they prefer not to kill if the US does pay). They will therefore kill if the US plays her dominant strategy and, since this gives the US government her first or second choice, not paying is the obvious US move. The outcome will be no pay/kill. There is no alternative outcome that is simultaneously preferred by both sides, so no deal seems likely. Forced to move first, the Iranians will kill, since if they don't, the US won't pay and will thereby guarantee the Iranians' least preferred solution.

This, of course, is the usual situation in which a government confronting this type of hostage crisis finds itself. It usually has nothing to lose by launching an all-out rescue attempt. It risks nothing when it risks the lives of the hostages, since there is no circumstance in which it is going to pay. (The chapter on hijacking discusses rescue missions more fully.)

The US media coverage of weeping relatives, however, quickly transformed distraught hostages into real people. This transformation had a critical impact on US preferences. It soon became clear that Carter would be in serious trouble if he 'allowed the hostages to die'. For periods during the crisis this meant that US preferences switched: pay/no kill was preferred to kill/no pay.

Such a change in US perceptions dramatically changes the game:

		Iranian students	
		No kill	Kill
US government	Pay	1st 2nd	2nd 4th
	No pay	4th 1st	3rd 3rd

US hostages in Iran: Phase Two

Both outcomes involving dead hostages appear at the bottom of the US government's list. The US still has a dominant strategy of not paying, but it is much less strongly dominant than that in the Phase One game. The critical point is that while no pay/kill is still the result of independent action by both sides, *each side* would prefer to see pay/no kill. The consequence of this is that each is prepared to deal with the other, and, if a deal can somehow be guaranteed, it will make both sides better off.

In practice, US government preferences probably vacillated between those of Phase One and those of Phase Two. The debate within the country focused on whether to emphasize foreign policy considerations (and therefore play the Phase One game) or to emphasize humanitarian concern for the hostages and their families (and therefore play the Phase Two game). Such a stark choice between two clear-cut outcomes is rare in politics. It provided considerable exercise for the Great American Conscience.

Given that a deal was on the cards if the US happened to be in a Phase Two mood at the time, it is interesting to explore the ways in which the students might have moved things along. The fact that they were holding a whole roomful of hostages gave them considerable leverage. A secret deal was ruled out by the tremendous worldwide interest. A public, *but conditional*, deal was clearly a possibility. If the students had been genuinely prepared to kill the hostages one by one, they might well have got what they wanted. Both sides might have arrived at a deal securing pay/no kill if the Iranians had shown that they were prepared to act in this way. The most serious drawback would have been the indivisibility of the Shah. If the ransom demand had been simply for money, there would have been no problem at all. The Iranians could have offered to release the hostages one by one, each in exchange for a portion of the cash. As soon as the US government didn't pay up on cue, a hostage could have been executed. The amount of the ransom that was outstanding could then have been reallocated among the remaining live hostages. As we shall see later on, killing any hostages can often provoke a desperate response from the victim in the form of a rescue mission. This time, as events showed, a rescue mission was virtually a technical impossibility.

The student's great weakness, therefore, was their inflexible demand for the return of the Shah. It is always possible that they could have broken up his release into thirty or so small stages, each insignificant in itself. He *could* have been moved a few miles at a time, but the crucial point at which he left US jurisdiction under duress would probably have been the stumbling block. Since the Shah was all the students really wanted, and since they really wanted him in one piece, the theoretical possibility of breaking up the negotiations into conditional stages did not really help them.

In practice, the result was predictable. Neither side wanted to make a move, and neither wanted the other to move first. The Iranian students couldn't move first because, if they did, they could only kill the hostages. This would have guaranteed that the Shah would not have been returned by the US government, and it was their third choice. If the students had released the hostages, the US government would not have given the Shah back, and the Iranians would have got their last choice. Forced to move first, the students had to make a move that guaranteed that the US would not pay. Carter's advisers almost certainly decided early on that the Iranians were not going to make the first move. At this stage the best hope for the US was to hang on and hope that something would turn up. The Shah, after all, was in bad health. The Ayatollah might have been overthrown. Since the Iranians were not going to take the first move, the US had the option of refusing to move as well and allowing the *status quo*, deadlock, to persist. Since deadlock was better than either giving in or losing the hostages, it was the best choice for the US. The US had no incentive to make a move. Why, however, did the Iranians not *force* the US to make a move by setting a deadline?

There seem to be three explanations for this: uncertainty, incompetence or a *really* burning desire to get the Shah back on

Iranian soil. Forcing the US to move first would have guaranteed a result for the Iranian students only if they could catch Carter in a Phase Two mood. Bear in mind that the soft-line Phase Two mood was the result of media pressure; it was not the natural response of a pro victim, which is to sacrifice the hostages in the cause of credibility. An ultimatum might have changed media attitudes to reinforce government inclination towards a hard line; it might not. Setting an ultimatum was a gamble that might or might not have worked. The problem, from the point of view of the students, was that there was only one Shah, and if the gamble had failed to pay off, their new-found credibility would have done them little good. Alternatively, they may simply have failed to appreciate the bargaining value of a serious deadline or knew that when the chips were down they would not implement it. The fact remains that, with a cluster of hostages, a threat to kill a hostage at regular intervals if the Shah was not returned might well have worked. Yet it was not attempted. Once the Shah died, the way was open for some hard dealing. It was then that the Iranians really failed to exploit their position. A conditional deal based on releasing hostages one by one was possible and could have made them big money.

Those who kidnap for money don't suffer the same constraints. Cash has the advantage of being almost infinitely divisible, allowing for all manner of conditional deals. Once you have a roomful of hostages, you can simply sell them back one at a time. This dispenses with the need for a middle-man or an ingenious method of making the switch. Each side quickly comes to trust the other because each needs the other.

The deal is quite straightforward. Say you have ten hostages and want a straight million for them. You can offer to release each one on receipt of a hundred thousand from the victim. You make it clear that if the instalment is not received on time, not only will one hostage be executed but the outstanding portion of the ransom will increase the instalments payable for the remaining live hostages. This little precaution is necessary to guard against the attempt of a mean victim to save some money by failing to pay for hostages he does not much like. It is no protection against a victim who actually wants some of the hostages dead, of course.

The victim has good reason to trust you and to make the first payment. If you do not release the hostage concerned, he has no incentive to make further payments. Knowing this, you should release the hostage. Knowing that you know this, he should pay in the first place. Once you have released a hostage, you have no incentive to kill hostages to protect your identity; the damage has been done. However, you do have an incentive to kill to enhance your credibility. This will give you a better chance of getting paid later in the day. Knowing that you know this, the victim should pay up, even if he thinks of you as a Nice Freelance. Thus by dealing with a whole group of hostages *any* kidnapper, be he Nice or Nasty Freelance or Pro, can take on the enormous bargaining advantage of the pro. With this sort of conditional deal, honouring each stage is crucial to a satisfactory conclusion. Everybody knows this, and thus everyone has an incentive to play it straight.

Even if the deal starts to go wrong, it should be self-regulating. Say the victim misses a payment. You have no choice but to kill the appropriate hostage. Having killed one hostage, you have nothing to lose by killing others. Since the demand now increases for the remaining hostages, the victim has saved no money. Your credibility is enhanced; the victim has gained no advantage. He may try this once, just to make sure you mean what you say, but after that he has every incentive to toe the line.

This looks an almost unbeatable venture, provided that you really are prepared to kill the hostages. You will be killing them for money, unlike the case of the lone hostage, whom you killed for credibility. It will be necessary to make sure that the hostages are well hidden, since the forces of law and order are apt to launch very intensive operations when hostages start dying one by one. In short, the extra inconvenience of having to kidnap and imprison a *group* of hostages is well rewarded by increased bargaining power and hence by extra cash.

HOW TO WIN AT KIDNAPPING

Kidnapping offers scope for freelance operators, unlike almost all of the other ventures that we will be discussing. It is not, however, a profession for softies. The successful kidnapper is the one who is perfectly prepared to kill the hostage and who can get this point across to his victim. In the protection business only the professional operator has any incentive to carry out the threat: to enhance his credibility. The twist in the kidnapping plot arises from an added incentive to carry out the threatened execution — the desire to destroy the evidence and reduce the risk of capture and conviction.

For an operator with no credibility at stake, this incentive to destroy the evidence causes as many problems as it solves, though the end result *may be* a payoff. A freelance's desire to kill his hostage is not *conditional* on his being paid. (The pro, who wants to make the same threat and promise again, is as keen to enact a promise not to kill as a threat to kill.) This reduces the incentive of a victim to pay a freelance unless some deal.can be arranged that is guaranteed by an outsider. Both kidnapper and victim are made better off by such a deal, and it is here that the scope for professional intermediaries arises. (The very best way to win at kidnapping is to become a professional intermediary.)

The unpredictable way in which a professional victim can react to the potential death of a hostage, and the influence of media coverage of such perfect stories of human tragedy, can combine to turn hardened pro victims into freelances. The possibility of kidnap insurance also reduces the determination of a pro victim to resist, especially if an offer of secrecy can be made and believed.

In short, not only does kidnapping offer the freelance the possibility of success but it also offers all comers almost their only serious hope of getting a fat payoff from a professional victim.

4

Blackmail

You may recollect being photographed 10 months ago at Maidenhead. These photographic negatives, which are in my possession, were to say the least very personal and should be of greatest interest to you. If such is the case you will reply to me, as you might like to regain possession of them.

I think some people will be very interested to hear what you are up to with your friend. Unless you pay £150 by tomorrow, I shall give your wife the whole story. Give your friend the money. She will know where to take it. Do not think I am joking. I have already told your friend's husband some things about you, so pay up.

I am very anxious to go abroad, but I require the necessary sum to make this possible. I want exactly £500. You will meet my agent tomorrow, April 10, at the lounge at the Strand Palace Hotel and wear two red carnations in your buttonhole. This sounds rather cheaply criminal, but it really is essential, and you will hand my agent a packet containing the sum of £250 in notes of £5. I will not be present and without the money is handed to me within half an hour after the time mentioned I will immediately make it my business to notify several folk in Eastbourne of the circumstances and as far as I can see your name will be drawn through the mud. This I know is against the law, but I want to leave the country and the sooner I go the better for all concerned.

Three letters written by Cosmo Brown

Dec. 1, 1886.
My dear Lord —

Unless you send £100 before Friday 7 pm to below address I shall communicate something to Sir Charles Russell which will surprise him, and the result of which will surprise you. Money in Bank of

England notes must be there by Friday. It will be of no use to send before to try and take proceedings against me as I shall not be there.

Yours
M. D. D.

P.S. If you want to win your case, my evidence had best be unheard. Take the hint.

Extracts from M. Hepworth, *Blackmail*, London, Routledge and Kegan Paul, 1975

THE EMBARRASSING CASE OF THE POLAROID PICTURES

It seemed like a good idea at the time. JJ and his boss, Ms Johnson, had been working their way through the *Kama Sutra* for several months. When she asked him to come along to a conference on new techniques in inflation accounting, he couldn't resist rushing out and buying a remote control for his trusty Polaroid. JJ had always been a keen photographer. The *Kama Sutra* went as well as ever and the remote control worked like a dream. The pictures were smashing. Every time Ms Johnson shouted at her secretary, he would pull them out of his wallet and feel better just looking at them. Then he lost the wallet.

JJ was a smart boy, and he did well. Ms Johnson was a big help. Soon he was up for the post of inflation accountant himself, with only the Snivelling Blenkinsop to beat. That's when it happened. Blenkinsop snivelled into his office one morning, toting something that looked a lot like JJ's lost wallet. SB had a cleft palate and made a lot of mess when he spoke, but JJ was able to make out something about Polaroid pictures and promotion prospects. There was also something about a cheque for four grand needed by SB to pay a plastic surgeon. Eventually Blenkinsop wrote it all down. It turned out that if JJ didn't immediately give him four grand, the Polaroids would end up in the hands of either God Almighty or the Managing Director (which for JJ amounted to pretty much the same thing.)

JJ is over a barrel. He accuses Blenkinsop of blackmail.

Puffing himself up into a fit of righteous indigestion, he explains that blackmail is illegal and immoral. He tries to scare SB by threatening to call the cops. SB shrugs his tiny shoulders and goes back to work. JJ doesn't pick up the phone.

It's not even as if JJ has committed any crime. The *Kama Sutra* is a perfectly legal sort of book, and Ms Johnson is a consenting adult, even if she is married to the Managing Director. But he knows that something dreadful will happen if any flatfoot gets hold of those photos. God Almighty is sure to find out. On the other hand, even if he does the deal, SB is sure to keep copies of the more revealing poses. He can drag them out again the next time he needs money for an operation. Blenkinsop can never be trusted. All that JJ can rely on is cowardice, indecision, malevolence and greed. Quite how that little stew of emotions will affect the blackmailer's guts in the coming weeks is anyone's guess. There's a good chance he won't have the nerve to go through with it. There's a good chance he will. If he doesn't get his rotten four grand, posting the pictures to Mr Johnson won't help him. But can he think that straight?

As blackmail victim, JJ has the two basic options: to pay up or stand up. (He would, of course, like to put out a contract on Blenkinsop but isn't wise enough in the ways of the world to know how to go about this). Having made the threat, the blackmailer has two choices: to publish or keep quiet. If he publishes, that is the end of it. If he keeps quiet now, he can always publish at some time in the future. The fact that a blackmailer always retains the option to publish in the future makes his occupation a little more complex than either kidnapping or extortion. Modern technology has ensured that anyone can easily make excellent copies of any prurient materials that might be in his possession. It is inconceivable that any blackmail interaction is ever really over until the smut is published and the blackmailer put behind bars or, better, left with a bullet in his back. Even if he promises on his grandmother's grave that he hasn't made a single copy, how can anyone believe him? The smut is his protection, and copies of it stashed in some safe place can do him no harm, even if he never needs to use them. They may provide a further source of income or, at the very least, force the victim to refrain from bringing down any heat. There is no possible advantage in *not* keeping copies (although there is considerable mileage in convincing the victim that none has been made).

JJ must therefore assume that he is never going to get back every single copy of his photos of Ms Johnson. This means that the only guaranteed ending to the game is to stand up and publish them himself, thereby rendering SB's copies of the pictures worthless. Otherwise Blenkinsop can always publish, whether JJ pays him or not. Once the money has been paid, the blackmailer can satisfy his malevolent urges by posting the prints anyway. Dealing with a blackmailer is not like dealing with a kidnapper. At least you know when you have got the hostage back home. You can never be sure about retrieving all the blackmail materials. Even if JJ convinces Blenkinsop that he is never going to pay, publication can add a bit of spice to offset the financial failure of the deal. The game therefore looks like this:

		SB (blackmailer)	
		No publish	Publish
JJ (victim)	Pay	$+4000$ * -4000	$+4000$ $+ x - h$ $-40,000$
	No pay	0 * 0	$+ x - h$ $-36,000$

$*$ = Both sides also take a gamble on playing the game again.

SB vs. JJ in the Polaroid shakedown

In this game JJ, the aspiring inflation accountant, first works out the value, at today's prices, of the promotion he will lose if the Polaroids are published. The promotion is worth 6000 a year for life. Inflation is eating this away at the rate of 20 per cent a year, so the total present value of his promotion is 36,000. Of course, if JJ pays the four-grand ransom and the pictures are published, he loses 40,000 altogether. Blenkinsop gets his 4000 if JJ pays up and nothing if he doesn't. On top of this, he gets a vicious thrill if the pictures are published, whether he gets paid or not. X is the malevolence factor.

To set against this there is the heat that will be generated if JJ calls the cops. If the pictures are published, JJ has no reason to call the cops, so both outcomes involving publication also involve heat. If JJ doesn't pay and Blenkinsop doesn't publish, there is no incentive to call the cops, and there may well be considerable mileage for JJ in keeping them out of things. H is the heat factor.

Finally, we see that if the pictures aren't published, there is some chance that they will both find themselves playing the same game again. The asterisk in each of the 'no publish' boxes indicates this. What happens?

For the moment, forget the prospect of a repeat performance. In this case JJ has a dominant strategy. This is not to pay. If Blenkinsop publishes, then JJ loses his promotion and the ransom (40,000) by paying, and 'only' his promotion (36,000) by not paying. If Blenkinsop doesn't publish, then JJ loses nothing (0) by not paying and loses the ransom (4000) by paying.

Blenkinsop has a dominant strategy too, though quite what this is will depend on how he compares the joys of malevolence with the costs of heat. If he feels really malevolent and reckons he can get away with it, his dominant strategy is publishing the pictures whether he is paid or not. This is because x is greater than h, yielding a malevolence bonus (m). (In the algebra of blackmail, $x > h$ and $x - h = m$.) Publishing yields 4000 plus the malevolence bonus if he's paid, and the malevolence bonus rather than nothing if he's not. The game will be as shown at the top of p.97.

If SB is not quite as vicious or even if he simply wants the money and is not vicious at all, then his dominant strategy will be no publish. The heat factor, h, will exceed the

	SB (blackmailer)	
	No publish	Publish
JJ (victim) — Pay	2nd / 2nd	1st / 4th
JJ (victim) — No pay	4th / 1st	3rd / 3rd

A malevolent blackmail situation

malevolence factor, x, yielding a heat deficit, q. ($h>x$, $h-x=q$) If JJ doesn't pay, then SB gets only the heat deficit if he publishes but no heat if he doesn't. If JJ does pay, the costs of the heat deficit must be deducted from SB's payoff — if he publishes, that is. The game is:

	SB (blackmailer)	
	No publish	Publish
JJ (victim) — Pay	1st / 2nd	2nd / 4th
JJ (victim) — No pay	3rd / 1st	4th / 3rd

A more mercenary blackmail situation

The most important thing for JJ to remember is that the Snivelling Blenkinsop is going to have a dominant strategy either way. For all practical purposes, this means that publication of the embarrassing Polaroids does not depend upon payment.

If SB is really in it for the money, the result is clear. JJ doesn't pay, while SB keeps quiet. Neither side gains a cent.

No heat, no embarrassment and JJ gets promoted. If the blackmailer has a chip on his shoulder, then paying him won't stop publication. Both sides have a dominant strategy once more, and the result is no pay/publish. This results in heat, embarrassment and no promotion for JJ. It is worse for both sides than pay/no publish. The trouble is that the order of the moves is not relevant. JJ can't avoid the sordid revelations by prompt payment. If JJ moves first, SB publishes regardless.

There is clearly scope here for a middle-man. Someone who can guarantee a deal would enable the two sides to come to an arrangement that was to their mutual advantage. If both sides can contract to the pay/no publish strategies, and if a third party was prepared to enforce the contract, for a fee, both blackmailer and victim are better off. If neither knows how to bring in such a middle-man, they are on a collision course. If SB is feeling vicious, the encounter will end in disaster, though the blackmailer will salvage the malevolent satisfaction of publishing the pictures.

Now, consider what happens if Blenkinsop keeps copies of the sordid photos. Even if he gives JJ the originals and doesn't publish, the copies can be used to make more demands in the future. If SB is a mercenary blackmailer and JJ knows this, the copies won't make SB any extra cash in years to come. JJ won't pay, and, once he has kept his nerve the first time and refused to pay, there is no reason why he should crack in the future. There is no percentage in Blenkinsop's making a second demand. However, if the snivelling blackmailer is vicious as well as greedy, or if JJ isn't prepared to take the risks, things are rather different and much more complicated.

Imagine, for the sake of argument, that JJ is quite overwhelmed by horror at Mr Johnson's likely reaction to seeing his wife in such a series of compromising positions. He cracks and pays. Blenkinsop, nasty piece of work that he is, is inclined to go right ahead and publish anyway. But if he does, he gives up the chance to demand more cash in the future. JJ has cracked once; there is no reason to suppose he won't crack again, provided that the price is not too high.

Blenkinsop may well make more money if he doesn't publish. Say that he could squeeze 4000 a year out of JJ if he holds on to at least one copy of the pornographic Polaroids. With inflation at 20 per cent, 4000 a year is worth a grand total of 24,000 at today's prices, before its value is completely eroded. If pay/no publish is worth twenty-four grand, he would have to be extraordinarily malevolent to prefer 4000 plus the vicious pleasure of publication that results from pay/publish. The game becomes:

		SB (blackmailer)	
		No publish	Publish
JJ (victim)	Pay	+24,000 −24,000	+4000 + x − h −40,000
	No pay	0 0	x − h −36,000

A far-sighted but malevolent blackmailer puts the squeeze on JJ

This has the structure:

		SB (blackmailer)	
		No publish	Publish
JJ (victim)	Pay	1st 2nd	2nd 4th
	No pay	4th 1st	3rd 3rd

The same thing

Blenkinsop no longer has a dominant strategy. Being a malevolent sort of fellow, he prefers publishing if JJ doesn't pay. Since the malevolence factor is not worth twenty grand, however, he prefers not to publish even if JJ pays. This will give him a steady source of income and will leave open the option of publishing at some later date. Now that SB has no dominant strategy, it is in JJ's interest to pay up quickly. He should realize that he will be blackmailed for the rest of his life, but, provided the blackmailer asks for a ransom that is lower than the cost of the damage that he can inflict, the victim must pay. JJ loses no time in paying because this guarantees pay/no publish rather than no pay/publish, which is what happens if he refuses to co-operate.

So the fact that the blackmailer can always keep a copy of the embarrassing materials does help him make money, provided that he is vicious enough to go ahead and publish if he doesn't get paid. Paradoxically, this also helps the victim. Faced with a malevolent blackmailer who keeps no copies, the likely outcome, as we have seen, is disaster. JJ loses 36,000 (with no pay/publish) if the malevolent Blenkinsop doesn't keep copies of his exploits with Ms Johnson, but he only loses 24,000 (with pay/no publish) if the copies are made and used. The hold that the blackmailer has over his victim enables them to arrive at the pay/no publish outcome they both prefer.

This assumes that the blackmailer pitches his regular demand low enough for the victim to think that it is worth while to keep on paying rather than to suffer the big initial loss that would result from exposure and scandal. Precisely how a blackmailer should calculate this demand will depend on whether the dirt he has on his victim would cause a single catastrophic loss or would sustain a continuous level of suffering. If the suffering is likely to be continuous, the demands must be calculated always to be rather less painful than the cost of exposure. Thus Blenkinsop asks for four thousand a year in exchange for allowing JJ to get a promotion worth six thousand a year. If the loss would be a single catastrophic event, such as the cancellation of a contract or grievous bodily harm inflicted by an irate spouse, the calculation is more complex. The periodic demand must be pitched so that the value of all future payments, given inflation, is less than the loss. Any competent firm of accountants should be well placed to advise on this. For those who are too shy or too mean to seek professional help, the table of blackmail accountancy should provide some rough rules of thumb. The table should help aspiring blackmailers to get a feel for the sort of regular demand they can safely make. Say, for example, that you come across information that would prevent a certain person from winning a ten-grand prize for being Ms. Whiter-than-White 1984. If inflation is 10 per cent per annum, the victim should be happy to pay you 800 a year forever. (The table shows that it is better to pay 800 a year forever than to lose 10,000 now.) If Ms. Whiter-than-White's horizon doesn't stretch that far in the future (so that she doesn't even think of payments made more than ten years from now), you can ask for much more. (The sum would be more than 2100 a year in this case.)

BLACKMAIL ACCOUNTANCY

Inflation rate (%)	Total value of 1000/yr forever at today's prices (to nearest 50)	Level of annual demand that, at today's prices, is 10% better than a fixed loss of 1000* (to nearest 5)
5	21,000	45
10	11,000	80
15	7,650	115
20	6,000	150
30	4,350	210
50	3,000	300
100	2,000	450
500	1,250	720
1000	1,100	810

* That is, annual demand that has a present value of 900 at today's prices, given the inflation rate indicated.

Assume that both sides stop thinking about future demands when inflation has reduced these to less than 1 per cent of their value at today's prices.

This schedule of blackmail demands is *very* conservative, in the sense that no victim will conceivably object to paying the sums indicated, even if he looks right ahead to the day of his death. Some people don't think quite so far ahead, and they can be made to pay for this lack of foresight. The shorter the victim's time horizon, the higher the demand. The skilled blackmailer will develop a feel for such matters, but the schedule is strongly recommended for beginners. It is fail-safe.

It can also be seen from the table that everyone involved in blackmail should be very sensitive to the prevailing level of inflation. A sudden drop in inflation can upset the most subtle blackmail arrangement. The victim may decide that the demand will now cost more than having embarrassing details spread all over the Sunday newspapers. Blackmailers should be more sensitive than most to the state of the economy. A subscription to a reputable financial journal is clearly indicated.

All of this only works if the blackmailer is prepared to go ahead and publish if he is not paid off. Payment depends upon the malevolence factor, x. Since a certain amount of blackmail is, so to speak, in the family, malevolence is plausible enough. When blackmail is engaged in purely for financial gain, the dominant strategy for the blackmailer is not to publish. The freelance mercenary blackmailer will not make a living squeezing a rational victim who keeps his nerve. Just as the freelance kidnap victim must decide whether the kidnapper is Nice or Nasty, the freelance blackmail victim must decide whether the blackmailer is malevolent or mercenary. This uncertainty puts pressure on the victim and may often result in a payout to a mercenary freelance that is made simply because the victim is not prepared to run the risk of guessing wrong.

BLACKMAIL AS A CAREER

Professional blackmail should be lucrative, provided that the blackmailer values his reputation. Like the pro racketeer and kidnapper, he will make money by earning the respect of potential victims. He will do this by being prepared to carry out threats, even at a short-term loss and solely in order to encourage the others:

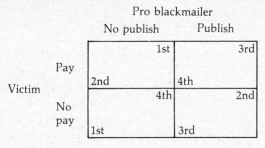

Professional blackmail

The deal offered by the professional blackmailer must be honoured at all costs, and the deal is pay/no publish or no pay/publish. The problem of demands continuing into the future also vanishes. This aspect will presumably be covered by the deal. If the pro promises no further demands, the promise should be kept. Indeed, the business of professional blackmail is so similar to that of professional kidnapping that we need not discuss it further.

CALLING THE COPS

JJ clearly doesn't call the cops because he has made up his mind that the Snivelling Blenkinsop is both far-sighted and malevolent. He decides to pay up, and the cops can do nothing to help. The victim of a pro blackmailer will make the same decision. In this respect, professional blackmail enjoys the same advantages as other strategic professions. The victim, faced with an offer he can't refuse, is forced to collude with the blackmailer, not only by paying up as quickly as possible but also by conspiring to exclude the police. The essential dilemmas are very similar to those facing the victims of extortion or kidnapping.

The cops, however, will get even less of a look-in with blackmail than they will with kidnapping because the blackmail victim, by definition, fears publicity above all else. It will be very difficult for the police credibly to guarantee that there will be no publicity, since any success they have in apprehending the villain is likely to result in a public court case. As dirty detail after dirty detail is laid bare by the lawyers, nobody will be fooled for very long about the identity of 'Mr A'. A kidnap victim who calls the cops will want them to succeed and will be prepared to pay their price, which is co-operation in bringing the perpetrator to justice. The kidnap victim facing a freelance kidnapper will call in the cavalry. As we have seen, he has nothing to lose and everything to gain. The blackmail victim facing a freelance blackmailer will have little to gain and a lot to lose by involving the police. If the blackmailer is caught, the worst is likely to happen, and his sordid secrets will adorn the front pages of the gutter press.

Successful police action might be as bad as the worst thing that can happen. If the blackmailer is not caught, there is no point in calling the cops in the first place. While the police will no doubt promise to protect the identity of the victim if he co-operates, and while they will no doubt attempt to do this (they have nothing to lose by protecting him), the risks of identification after a public court case must always weigh heavily on the victim's mind.

This problem will be especially acute when the victim is being blackmailed for illegal activities. The fear of going to the police is then not that the whole affair becomes public knowledge (a hardened criminal may not give a damn about this) but that the *police* will get to hear about it. (This is, when you think about it, more or less inevitable.) The end-product may well be prosecution and prison for the victim as well as the blackmailer. Obviously, the police have an incentive to promise some sort of protection for blackmail victims, otherwise victims will be very reluctant to use them, and blackmailers will prosper. They may even, in practice, offer some immunity from prosecution for minor offences. (If you try to make me pay up by threatening to tell the police about that red light I ran this morning, they'll probably let me off and throw you in the slammer.) But they're going to draw the line somewhere. They won't let you off a murder rap just because you're being blackmailed. Indeed, murderers look to be almost perfect victims.

One possibility is for the police to take out the blackmailer in secret or, at the very least, for secret courts to be established for the purpose of hearing blackmail cases. General bourgeois principles of natural justice tend to interfere with these obvious solutions to the blackmail victim's dilemma, and the only alternative is the private enforcement system. Given the relative uselessness of the straight enforcement industry in matters relating to blackmail, the scope for private enforcement is considerable. If I were a blackmailer, the thing I would most fear is a bullet in the back.

THAT'S BLACKMAIL!

No, it isn't. Along with love and democracy, blackmail is a word that is much misunderstood and misused. The result is the loss of a valuable idea to the catch-all family of words used simply to indicate approval or disapproval. 'That's blackmail' usually means 'You're putting the screws on me and I don't like it.' 'If you don't give us a pay rise, we'll go on strike', 'If you go on strike, we'll close the company': both threats are often described as blackmail by the recipients when both are really forms of extortion. The victim has nothing to hide. 'If you don't give us a pay rise, we'll tell the world about your illegal dumping of toxic waste': now *that* looks a bit more like blackmail and seems, furthermore, to be an offer worth making during the course of a difficult industrial dispute. It may, of course, happen all the time, since neither would ever have an incentive to own up to making or agreeing to such an offer.

In the light of this confusion over the true nature of blackmail, a brief review of the essential strategic differences between it and extortion or kidnap is in order. Playing blackmail is a little like playing kidnap, except that the kidnap victim is held by either kidnapper or hostage, one or the other, but not by both at the same time. Blackmail materials can never be wholly returned to the victim, since the principal blackmail material is information. Information can be easily reproduced, invisibly stored inside a brain and destroyed only with the greatest difficulty. Once I possess a piece of information, the only certain way to destroy it is to destroy me or, at the very least, a large part of my brain. Aside from removing the blackmailer, blackmail information can only be fully neutralized by publication, at great cost to the victim.

In this respect, extortion and blackmail are similar. The extortionist threatens to damage the victim if money is not paid. Whatever happens, the possibility of damage can never be removed until the extortionist is eliminated. The difference between extortion and blackmail is the much greater reluctance of blackmail victims (especially criminal victims, the best sort) to involve the police.

In many ways, therefore, blackmail is the safest of the three crimes. Not only does it select the shyest victims but it also operates at arm's length. Given that the handover of the blackmail material can never be complete, once the victim has decided to pay, he pays first and waits for the result. He may be given something by the blackmailer, but this is, in a sense, irrelevant. He must assume that whatever he is given has been copied. This means that the technicalities of the transfer do not create problems, as they do with kidnapping. If it comes to carrying out the threat, the blackmailer can achieve this with a stamp and the help of the postal system. Nothing more is needed. This contrasts dramatically with kidnap and extortion, in which the enactment of the threat involves a close-quarters confrontation that can range from malicious damage to murder.

On the other side of this coin, the relatively safe enterprise of blackmail suffers from the problem that reputations tend to be worth less than bodies, and some reputations are worth nothing at all. Payoffs are smaller and more erratic. This is why kidnappers and extortionists tend to look down on blackmailers, regarding them as timid and small-minded. Many people, however, make a comfortable living doing things that are looked down on.

5

A short treatise on the economics of fear

Don Vanni replied in a letter apparently courteous but so charged with Mafia Symbolism that the priest had it interpreted by an expert before realizing that it contained a threat to hang him from his own church tower.

Norman Lewis, *The Honoured Society*, Harmondsworth, Penguin, 1967, pp.82−3

JACK THE LAD AND FLASH HARRY GO TO JAIL

Jack the Lad and Flash Harry are riding around in a shiny new stolen Jaguar. They usually choose a Jag or a Merc when it is raining, but this time they end up in the slammer. Being well-known to the local constabulary, things look bad. Worse still, there are heavy hints flying around about the bank job they pulled last Friday. Soon enough they are sitting in separate rooms sucking cigarettes thrown at them by two slimy young detectives. A deal is in the air. The filth can't pin a thing on them. They did a bank job sixty miles from home and haven't told a soul. Sawn-off shotguns and stocking masks made sure that the odd passer-by didn't take too close a look. But someone somewhere has smelt something.

After a lot of time spent trying to slither under Jack's honest car-thief act, Detective Number One gives up and blurts out the deal. 'We know you did the bank, but we can't make it stick. We want someone for that job, and we'll have Harry if you talk. Talk, and you walk out of here a free man. Don't talk and we'll throw two tons of stolen Jaguar at you. With your record, you'll do a year at least.' Now, Jack the

Lad has had conversations with detectives before. He knows they always hold back a little something. This rancid excuse for a human being has forgotten to mention what happens to Jack if he squeals and Harry does too. That way no one needs either of them, and they both take a ride for the bank job.

The Lad hasn't made it big enough to own a nice house in the suburbs by saying the first thing that comes into his head. He knows that this little proposition might not smell as bad as it did the first time he took the paper off. They wouldn't say they couldn't pin the bank job on him if they could, so they can't. They're going to be very aggravated if they don't do someone for that bank, so he wouldn't put it past them to give him a hard time over the Jag. If he signs the statement and they try to get him anyway, he can take it back and tell the judge they beat the confession out of him. A bruise or two here and there shouldn't be too hard to come by. So far so good.

But what about Flash Harry? If Harry signs too, they both go down. And Detective Number Two has, for certain, been laying out the same deal in the next room. This means that the cops are playing them off against each other. If they both keep quiet, both do a year for the stolen Jag. If they both talk, they both do eight years for the bank. If one talks and the other doesn't, the one who talks gets nothing, while the one who doesn't talk gets ten years, taking the whole blame and not even getting a year or two off for being helpful.

However Jack thinks about it, the only thing to do is talk.

		Flash Harry	
		No talk	Talk
Jack the Lad	No talk	1 1	0 10
	Talk	10 0	8 8

Jack's and Harry's dilemma, paid off in years in jail

He does better talking whether Harry talks or not. If Harry's been offered the same deal, he'll think the same way. But if they both talk, that's the worst thing that can happen, landing them each with eight years in the slammer. They'd both be *much* better off keeping quiet. But if one keeps quiet, the other is bound to talk and walk away a free man. Neither can take the risk.

Jack wishes he could have a word with Harry and point this out, until he realizes that it won't do any good. What happens when they get together and promise not to talk? The moment they are separated, each is going to be racing to rat on the other. There is absolutely nothing to lose by talking, even though if they both talk, they are both worse off. Talking gets you eight years rather than ten if the other guy talks, and no years rather than one if he doesn't. And that's that.

Jack the Lad and Flash Harry go to jail, but things could have been different. The Mob kills people who talk to detectives. They should join the Mob. This may seem like a harsh treatment for verbal diarrhoea, but the purpose is not to cure the disease but to prevent it. Nobody has to get killed because nobody talks and each is better off. If Jack and Flash Harry join an outfit like this, they'll face a very different dilemma the next time the filth pick them up in some stolen wheels. Certain death is added to some of the payoffs and sanity thereby restored. Now their decision looks like this:

Flash Harry

	No talk	Talk
Jack the Lad — No talk	1 / 1	0 + death / 10
Jack the Lad — Talk	10 / 0 + death	8 + death / 8 + death

Years in jail for Jack and Harry, who do their time and stay healthy

However they look at it, not talking looks by far the best bet. This is because, whatever the other guy does, talking guarantees certain death. *So neither talks, neither dies, and both end up better than if they hadn't joined the Mob.* Each does a year behind bars, to be sure, but there was never any real prospect of less. The fourteen years of freedom they save between them in a single brush with the forces of justice are well worth the high dues they have to pay for their membership. The neat little death threat lets everyone win, with the exception of the police, who don't catch any bank robbers.

THE ENFORCEMENT BUSINESS

Identifying the market

Jack the Lad and Flash Harry stay out of serious trouble by joining the Mob. The Mob stops them from double-crossing each other every time they feel like it and extends this service to anyone who gives evidence against its members. It is a very valuable service, and members are prepared to pay high dues. Killing grasses is potentially very lucrative, but it is just one small example of the profits to be made in the professional enforcement business.

It is a sad fact of business life that in certain lines of work people will double-cross you as soon as fart. When this happens, you have no one to turn to. If I go into business selling cars from a classy high street showroom, I can call in the legitimate legal muscle when Joe Soap writes a hot cheque for that brand new two-tone convertible. When I move on to selling nearly new, one-owner machines liberated from the local multi-storey car park it's no good snivelling along to the cops the first time a cheque bounces. Unless I sell only to customers with huge rolls of unmarked banknotes in their back pockets, I need to hire some new muscle. The cops, the judges and the lawyers have the straight enforcement business pretty well sewn up, but by taking a dim view of those of us who sell hot cars or hot pants, they've left a huge gap in the market. Every market needs some enforcers because no one can get anywhere if he can't do deals with people and be sure that those deals will be honoured.

There are basically two types of people who don't honour deals. First, some people are just plain dishonest. They make you promises that they never intend to keep. These deals are not really deals at all. They are frauds, designed to relieve you of your hard-earned cash. If people are allowed to get away with such dishonest behaviour, the whole business community gets a bad name, and it becomes almost impossible to make money. The market will grind to a near-halt if you can part with the money only at the instant you get the goods or vice versa. Even a simple little transaction like backing the favourite to win at your local race track will become almost impossible. You won't give the money to the bookie if you don't trust him. He won't take your bet without the money if he can't trust you. Neither of you will give the money to a stake-holder if he's liable to scarper. If no one can trust anyone else, the whole business of betting is a write-off. If people aren't naturally trustworthy, they must be *made* to be trustworthy, or life won't be worth living.

Secondly, some people are honest enough when they make a deal but just don't deliver the goods when their number is called. Sometimes this is because they are stupid, never could deliver the goods, but just didn't realize this. Sometimes unfortunate accidents can befall even the most intelligent of honest businessmen. Sometimes what looked like a good deal at the time looks pretty unattractive when the due date arrives. The stupid are no better than the crooks and need to be educated. Unfortunate accidents can be very unfortunate, but that's no reason why you shouldn't pay the price. Deals that don't look as good in the cold light of day as they did in last night's smoky bar room are what business is all about. If the stolen Jag you just bought for two grand turns out to need a new engine, you should have checked that out before you shook hands. A deal is a deal.

The trouble is that a deal is not a deal if it can't be enforced. Moreover, when we *really* get down to it, fear, force and pain are the only things that work. The policemen, lawyers and judges of the straight enforcement Mafia may claim that they left fear and pain behind a century or two ago. Not so. You run a red light, and you get a traffic ticket. This might look like a civilized little fine, but it's not — it's a threat. Don't pay the traffic ticket and they'll take you to court. Don't pay the fine in court and sooner or later you'll face a jail sentence. Don't go to jail and they'll force you. Resist and they'll hurt you. The *very, very* bottom line is always pain.

In those areas of business activity that are abandoned by the straight enforcement Mafia, there will still be a demand for pain. Pain and fear are valuable commodities, and lawyers and judges aren't the only ones who can supply it at a profit. If you decide to go into the business of supplying professional enforcement services, form a little company and call it something like Friendly Enforcement and Research Incorporated. You will need a business address, some publicity material and one or two operatives, who can, of course, be taken on as subcontractors. Above all, FEAR Inc. will need to project an impressive corporate image. All products and materials should be instantly and unmistakably recognizable.

You will already have identified your basic market, of course. This consists of all people who want to make deals. To avoid competition in the early stages of corporate expansion, you may well decide to ignore those people who make deals that can be enforced by the established enforcement industry, concentrating on the pimps, hustlers, fences, bookies and others who are not inclined to try to enforce their deals in courts of law. The basic product line could hardly be more simple. In exchange for a fat fee, the purveyor of hot cars can rent a large notice to hang in his showroom. This informs clients that all deals made on the premises are guaranteed by FEAR Inc. These notices are cheap to print but extremely valuable to those who rent them. They are thus a perfect product line. The notice is backed up by FEAR's commercial conciliation and arbitration service, to which all trade disputes must be referred. As with many things, huge savings of the expenses incurred by the otherwise similar but cumbersome state system can be achieved. All forms of appeal can be dispensed with, since FEAR's decisions are final. Modern and efficient forms of punishment, such as bone-breaking, mutilation and death, replace the tiresome and expensive system of penal servitude used by the old fashioned police — lawyer — judge enforcement oligopoly. (As we have already seen, penal servitude depends on fear in the final analysis. FEAR simply cuts through unnecessary red tape.) Since specialists in the application of extreme physical pain need a far shorter training period than lawyers and judges, and since the certainty of two broken legs is a more effective deterrent to business irregularity than a long law suit (which might always be won), costs can be kept low. Notwithstanding low costs, and because of the more efficient service it provides, FEAR offers a better deal to the customer than its public-sector competition. High prices can be maintained, therefore, and the business should be extremely profitable.

The scope for expansion is enormous. In the early days the market will include all businessmen engaged in activity that they are attempting to conceal from the police. When Jack the Lad borrows money to buy the thermal lance he needs to get into a particularly tough safe, he is much more likely to pay it back if FEAR is brought in to guarantee the deal. The same night he is more likely to pay the hooker with a FEAR sticker over her bed, the dealer selling FEAR-protected coke or the salesman with the stolen two-tone convertible. Everyone benefits. The business community gets its money, and Harry doesn't have to carry huge wads of stolen cash around before he can persuade anyone to part with the goods.

On top of businessmen who want to avoid any cops who might take an unwelcome interest in their merchandise, there will be many who are simply impatient. Taking people to court is an expensive gamble, which carries nothing like the guarantee that FEAR can provide. You may be selling goods that you would be happy to wave under the noses of a thousand policemen but still prefer to pay the high costs of a FEAR policy because it gets results. You run a small slot machine operation, for example, and suspect the owners of your sites to be skimming the profits. This is downright illegal of them, and they will be rapped over the knuckles by the bench if you can ever get hold of the evidence. When you *know* they are skimming, however, getting all that evidence is a boring waste of time. FEAR can be brought in to solve the problem more efficiently, starting with a quiet word in the ear and moving on swiftly to an iron bar in the neck. They're expensive, but that greasy mouthpiece you hire to represent you in court wouldn't be cheap either. In short, 'legitimate' businessmen will want to employ FEAR for those little jobs the police so often bungle.

The corporate image

FEAR's image is crucial. This is because the company is, in effect, involved in an innovative new aspect of public relations, and the image of a public relations company is its shop window. No one is going to take on a PR firm whose own image is a mess. No one is going to take on a contract enforcement agency that doesn't look pretty scary. One concept, omnipotence, must pervade FEAR's corporate profile. Businessmen are not going to shell out hard cash for some Mickey Mouse operation that wouldn't scare the shit out of a sub-postmistress. They *will* pay big money for an organization that has customers falling over themselves to pay their bills.

If FEAR is going to scare people that badly, it needs either a medium-sized army or a red-hot reputation. A reputation is much cheaper and much safer. When you start in the enforcement business, you will have to hunt down every small-time chiseller who breaks the rules and make each one very sorry. A lot of pain will have to be inflicted in the early days. Distasteful though this may be, it pays off in the long term. The sorrier you make them today, the quicker they learn to toe the line, and the less pain you will have to inflict in the future. Anyway, the pain is for their own good. If people don't pay their bills, then the business community of this city will go to the wall and no one is going to be able to buy a hot car or a bag of dope, a .357 magnum or a warm bed. Then where would we all be? The valuable public service provided by contract enforcers must be exploited in all image-building activity. You may have set up FEAR in order to make a lot of money, but there is no reason why you should admit this in public. The message that FEAR is good for people must be rammed home at every opportunity.

To begin with, Friendly Enforcement will need at least a small army, but once your image of speedy and efficient service is established, 90 per cent of the soldiers can be pensioned off. After that only the newcomers and a few old-timers with short memories will need any electric drill therapy. By this stage, FEAR is selling an image as much as a product. The market is much more likely to expand into new territory if you don't have to hurt too many clients. Your ultimate objective should be to make the service you provide invisible yet hugely valuable. This, of course, is the position of all of the really large international companies. Cosmic Drinks, after all, makes its money selling a worldwide corporate image stuck on to some fizzy water coloured with caramel. These days you can hardly find a thirsty person who can tell you what a Cosmic Drink tastes like, yet they all know it's just what they need. If you succeed in imposing an image of effortless omnipotence, an entirely new and vastly lucrative market will open up. There are too many operators in what we can think of as the fuddy-duddy business community, and there are several fortunes to be made by getting around all the red tape that is the bane of the modern businessman's existence. The FEAR motto 'Problems solved' will appeal to the buccaneering young entrepreneur this country needs so much. In some fields, such as property rental and gambling, there are already consultancies that specialize in the encouragement of difficult clients. The scope, however, is limitless. Which businessman doesn't have enemies and doesn't dream of their falling under buses or slipping and breaking both their legs before an important meeting? FEAR can turn these dreams into reality, in discreet if expensive style, with carefully protected reputations and a chain of salesmen who can always be contacted by everyone who is anyone. Troublesome tax inspectors, city officials, local councillors, union leaders and competitors can be removed at the stroke of a pen, and the prices they are likely to fetch will dwarf the odd couple of grand that can be picked up by straightening out a small-time pusher.

Competition policy

Every businessman loathes competition. Nothing is more galling than taking the trouble to develop a lucrative new market and then having some smart alec move in and make all the money! Competition means reduced profits, and reduced profits are not what businessmen are in business to make. Heaven for an up-and-coming young businessman is to have 100 per cent monopoly control over the water and air supplies of a large continent. Failing this, he never forgets the simple fact of economic life that the price he can charge for a product lies somewhere between what he is prepard to supply it for and what the customer is prepared to pay. There is often a very big gap between these two figures, particularly when he supplies a very valuable product, such as contract enforcement, which can be produced very cheaply. As soon as he is charging less than the customer is prepared to pay, he is throwing money down the drain. That's the trouble with competitors. They undercut you. Those who have read textbooks on economics and think that they know how the market works seem to think that it works by charging a lower price than their rivals. They live in a fantasy world in which price cutting goes on to such an extent that producers end up selling goods for what it costs to produce them plus a modest profit. Money pours down the drain as consumers often get goods for less than they might be prepared to pay for them. Of course, shortages do occur in this Never-Never-Land, and when they do, prices rise. But shortages are always presented as if they were acts of God. So the wheat harvest fails because of some sunspot or other, and those lucky enough to have wheat find a nice fat profit dropping into their laps when prices rise. This ignores the fact that wheat harvests can be *made* to fail and that sitting around waiting for acts of God is a pretty lame way of making super-profits.

There are two basic problems with competitors, therefore. In the first place, they undercut you so that they can steal your customers; in the second place, they produce too much of whatever it is you supply and end up flooding the market. Every businessman has to face up to the problem of what to do about competitors. The textbook answer is to try to beat them at their own game. Textbooks, however, are wrong. Trying to beat a competitor at his own game is like trying to run up an accelerating downward escalator. You can't win. You undercut them, they undercut you back. Soon you end up giving the stuff away and go broke. This is what happens in Never-Never-Land. A more realistic variation on this is to chop your own prices so much that you force the opposition out of business by selling at a huge loss. To do this, you must be stronger than your rival. If you are, it works reasonably well, since prices can always be raised afterwards to recoup any short-term losses. Once you are the biggest and baddest operator in the market, this technique should help to keep you there. It has the advantage of being regarded as entirely legal by all and sundry and is admired by most people as smart business practice. It has the great disadvantage that it only works if you're already on top; it won't help you to get there.

The main alternative, non-violent answer to the problem of competition is to do a deal with your competitors. You can agree to fix prices and restrict supply. This is another example of smart business practice, though a trifle less legal in some systems than killing off competitors by lethal price wars. If you're determined to fix prices, however, there's very little that can be done about it, particularly if you're smart. The most obvious technique is for each price fixer to offer a bewildering product range with all sorts of minor variations, bells and whistles, so that none actually markets exactly the same product. This way, price comparisons can always be plausibly undermined. The enormous disadvantage of price fixing is that it involves sharing the market with competitors. If monopoly control can be established, you can enjoy their profits as well as your own.

Killer pricing and price fixing are *much* better than unrestrained competition but *much* worse than 100 per cent monopoly control. For the up-and-coming young business, by far the most effective method of acquiring this is the direct elimination of competition. Direct techniques level the odds, while traditional indirect techniques load them in favour of the market leaders. It is really remarkable that so few textbooks even mention the direct method of market regulation. Despite the fact that killing competitors is so much more efficient than any other method of getting rich, it seems to be regarded as beyond the Pale by even the most aggressive texts on economics (as getting rich is usually referred to in the trade).

Take, for example, the sort of problem that might face Friendly Enforcement and Research Inc. a few months after it has really made an impact on the enforcement market. An upstart operation, Professional Adjustment and Insurance Negotiators, moves in and offers a similar service at a lower price. FEAR salesmen are confronted by clients who mutter about the PAIN contract, which does seem cheaper and offers the added incentive of compensating customers for bad debts. PAIN still seems to be making buckets of money selling half-price contract guarantees. (Not only does it not have to finance a research and development programme, but FEAR's 2000 per cent mark-up allows plenty of scope for price cutting.)

If FEAR lowers itself by engaging in direct competition with PAIN, there is no knowing where things might end. FEAR may undercut PAIN for a time, but then prices will drop and drop as each has to beat the other. In the end, both will be forced to issue guarantees at little more than the cost price. At that stage FEAR executives might well be selling apples in the market place as running a big-time business enterprise.

The executive director of Friendly Enforcement could, of course, have talks with his opposite number at PAIN, with a view to carving up the market. PAIN prices could be raised to match those of FEAR, and PAIN could agree not to operate north of the river. This is better than out-and-out competition, but what happens the next time someone tries to muscle in? Another carve-up, in which case there will soon be nothing left to carve. Market-sharing cartels are a short-term solution but, as any oil company will tell you, they do nothing to discourage the others.

The only long-term solution for Friendly Enforcement is to smash Personal Adjustment and Insurance as soon as it appears. Without doubt, the most effective way to do this is to execute every PAIN executive. This not only leaves market share and profits intact but also discourages other greedy wide boys from getting big ideas. FEAR can easily look after itself, of course, having an effective implementation division experienced in such matters.

Having regulated competition in its own back yard, it should be clear that FEAR can offer competition regulation on a contract basis. Competition regulation should be an immensely attractive and lucrative market. This is because it possesses that magical property that makes for a successful business venture: it's cheap to produce, yet customers will be prepared to pay a lot for it.

Quite how easy it will be to regulate competition will depend on how far the market has been allowed to deteriorate before a reputable regulation agency is called in. As with many aspects of life on this planet, it is much easier to stamp out competition if it's caught in the early stages. Think of competitors as vermin. One rat can easily be disposed of with a simple trap or a single slug from a .22. An infestation of rats can be hard work, even with a tank. As it happens, competitors are worse than rats. A single competitor can spoil things for a pretty big-time operation. It only takes one person offering a cheaper deal for customers to be rushing away from you like frightened rabbits. Two competitors are hardly worse than one. If a market has deteriorated so far into the corruption of competition that there are several hundred producers, any regulation programme will be a long haul. You can exterminate a hundred, at considerable expense, and hardly notice the difference in the price level. Another hundred gone, and things are a little better. It's that last dead competitor that makes all the difference and adds all the value. Nipping competition in the bud is an immensely valuable regulation service that can be provided at little expense, though for huge fees.

The precise level of fees which can be charged (though not the costs involved) will depend critically on the nature of the market to be regulated.

Once more, the crucial factor is the size of the gap between what people are prepared to pay and what the commodity costs to supply. There are some things that people stop wanting pretty quickly as the price goes up. Take pocket calculators, for example. People are prepared to walk around with pocket calculators stuffed into every orifice if the price is right. Put the prices up a bit and you can hardly sell a single calculator to an accountant. But you can sell a glass of water at almost any price in the middle of the Sahara Desert. Competition regulation is going to be most effective in those product areas where people are not too sensitive to the price structure. Sex, drugs and alcohol are good examples, though sex and alcohol have the disadvantage that it is difficult to control the DIY market. Addictive drugs are perfect — they often cost next to nothing to produce yet are infinitely valuable to clients. Thus while it is possible to regulate the market in pocket calculators, this would be a waste of enforcement resources. A monopoly position could be established by eliminating competitors, but monopoly profits would be relatively low because people would stop buying calculators if the price were too high. Eliminating competitors in the drug market might cost no more but would be much more lucrative. The monopoly profits would be greater because consumers are less sensitive to price increases.

The two key decisions facing any regulation agency will

thus concern the number of competitive producers and the price sensitivity of consumers. Markets with few producers and insensitive consumers are ideal.

Sometimes governments do all the hard work for you. They ban things, like alcohol or hard-core pornography, for which there is a healthy demand. They fix artificially low prices for things in short supply (like petrol in an oil crisis). They ration them, regulate them and do all manner of other things that stop people with the money to pay from getting enough of what they want. This type of government intervention is good news for anyone concerned with competition regulation. It creates a market that is easy to control. Anyone who deals in this market will need private contract-enforcement services anyway, since he can have no recourse to the state sector. The entire business environment is tailor-made for an outfit with a powerful enforcement division. Better still, the forces of justice will usually help out by cracking down on the DIY sector, which is the bane of any businessman's life.

From all of this we can see that the key to successful competition regulation is enforcement. A successful and reputable implementation division, one of the sort developed by any worthwhile contract-guarantee company, should be well equipped to eliminate competition in key markets. In general, key markets will be those in which a successful cartel can operate. These can be more efficiently exploited by competition regulation based on the direct elimination of rival producers. Indeed, failure to deal with competition in this way can only result in a serious loss of profitability.

Joint ventures

By the time a business is well established as a contract guarantor and competition regulator, it will have developed considerable expertise in certain markets. It can, of course, sell this expertise, but a much more effective technique, well proven in recent years, is the franchise system. Contract enforcers and competition regulators trade on their reputation, their most valuable business asset. This asset can be made available, at a price, to other businesses. The most effective method of doing this is to set up a franchise or joint venture arrangement with the business concerned. Franchises or joint ventures will be more satisfactory when enforcement and regulation services are considered by some to be illegal. A deal between, for example, a construction company and an enforcement agency to eliminate or intimidate rival contractors will run some risk of being seen as a conspiracy to commit illegal acts. Payments may be hard to explain, and unnecessary heat can be guaranteed. These problems are solved if the enforcement agency goes into partnership with the construction company. No embarrassing payments need to be made, and the role of the enforcement agency does not need to be explained. If the agency is an established competition regulator, everyone who needs to know will be aware of the implications of the new partnership, and potential rivals will be appropriately circumspect about engaging in unfair competition and price cutting.

Say, for example, that Friendly Enforcement and Research Inc. publicly associates itself with the Neighbourhood Construction Company *and takes a sizeable share of NCC profits*. People will now take NCC much more seriously. Before the merger, NCC was just any old construction company, developing sites where it could, relying on the goodwill of suppliers and customers and having to recourse to expensive legal proceedings when this goodwill ran out. Every time a new project came up, NCC had to submit itself to the humiliation of pleading for planning permission from the city council, the expensive business of competitive tender for building sites, the nuisance of dealing with trade unions and so on. Too many construction companies sink under the weight of all this aggravation. Now Friendly's reputation for speedy and efficient service helps these problems to disappear. Goodwill among city officials, suppliers and union bosses soars to an all-time high. The NCC tender for that juicy site is accepted even when it is only one-tenth as big as the highest bid. Any problems that remain can be handed over to the FEAR implementation division. There may, of course, be a few disappearances and nasty accidents in the early days, while Friendly's reputation is establishing itself in its new environment. Before long, however, the implementation division will rarely be called on, and the business affairs of Neighbourhood Construction will be indistinguishable from those of any other company. It will, of course, make much more money, with all those easy planning permissions, cheap sites and prompt settlements of accounts. With such a startling upturn in profits, NCC shareholders can hardly complain about handing over 50 per cent of NCC equity to FEAR as a free gift.

The tremendous advantage of this arrangement for FEAR is that it is much less exposed to any heat that might be generated by some two-bit police chief who decides to make his name by cleaning up the city. Competition regulation and contract enforcement in the informal market involve a small element of risk. This is greatly reduced by grass elimination but never completely disappears. Some people regard hard-core, hot cars, and heroin as undesirable commodities, and some of this public disapproval is bound to rub off on anyone associated with them. While these are ideal markets for an up-and-coming enforcer still making his name, the name, once made, can be put to better use. Who can complain about a construction company that builds houses faster and more cheaply than anyone else, yet still makes huge profits? The directors are all good-living family men, even if each does tend to have an interesting past. The net effect is a stable and profitable commercial environment. The cost is a barely perceptible increase in the death rate.

Keeping things cool

The market can be a pretty rough place. A lot of local colour can be found in the company of loan sharks, hookers and cocaine salesmen. Most of this local colour is heavily armed and made up of individuals who are liable to cut up at the slightest provocation.

Just because a smidgeon of ultra-violence must be applied from time to time in the course of business, that does not mean that the whole commercial environment needs to descend into anarchy. Gratuitous violence is bad for business, bringing down a lot of heat from clean-up campaigners, police chiefs and other do-gooders. (All violence not sanctioned by the *bona fide* executives of an established contract enforcement and competition regulation agency is, by definition, gratuitous.) Any violence entails some small risk, and risk without profit equals commercial suicide. The answer, of course, is discipline.

A big-time enforcement syndicate will not have got where it is without being disciplined, and it won't stay where it is without disciplining others. The men of respect have traditionally shipped their hotheads to the New World, but with no New Worlds left, the Next One is the only alternative. Freelance operators in *direct* competition will already have been dealt with as a part of general competition-regulation policy. However, all operators, even when they do not represent a direct commercial challenge, must be closely watched. Those who do well now may represent a future threat, and they will be much more difficult to deal with when they are strong. Others may run around in far too flashy a manner and simply draw attention to aspects of market behaviour that are best pursued with the utmost discretion.

It's up to the market leaders to keep things cool. Since no market can operate in a state of chaos and disorder, successful contract enforcers and competition regulators bear a heavy social responsibility. Stepping into market areas abandoned by the straight enforcement industry, they have the resources and they have the obligation to impose discipline. They will need to do this *even when their commercial interests are not directly threatened*. If they do not intervene, no one else will, and commercial life will quickly become intolerable. If market-leading enforcers hold a narrow view of commercial self-interest, this will ultimately be self-defeating. Such organizations will therefore find the roles of judge, jury and executioner thrust upon them. In addition to the contract policing of clients' interests on straightforward commercial terms, other (possibly even *unpaid*) jobs may have to be undertaken. There is no need to waste money or effort on any complicated procedures. Cases such as these can be turned over to the implementation division for execution on slow days. In matters of public order, an effective syndicate will usually be much more successful than the legal establishment. At a time when you had to chain your car to a lamp post in downtown Rome, you could leave the keys in the ignition in Palermo, a city with a highly developed private enforcement sector.

The great advantage of this system of peace keeping, over and above its effectiveness, is the introduction of an element of competition. The state judicial industry controls an effective monopoly of straight enforcement. If you attempt to bring someone to justice and lose your case, there is little more that you can do. Without doubt, this lack of judicial competition contributes to the sluggish performance of the state sector, a sluggish performance demonstrated by low conviction rates and half-hearted punishment systems. Rival private enforcement agencies, attempting to develop and secure a reputation upon which all of their business activity depends, will doubtless be more efficient. Each agency knows that if a plaintiff does not get a result from one, he will turn to a competitor and try again. Worse, once word gets around of poor results, the supply of plaintiffs will dry up altogether. This should keep all on their toes and conviction rates high. Efficiency will therefore increase. In addition, there is the added bonus of increased consumer choice, which is, of course, a good in its own right.

COLLUSION POLICY

Territories

So far, I have been overoptimistic. Competition regulation will rarely be so successful that a single operation will be the only one doing business. Most will be forced to share the market with others who simply have too big an arsenal to be dealt with effectively by direct methods. This will usually be the result of either a flaw in early business strategy or a late entry into the market, but such problems must be confronted.

Friendly Enforcement and Research, having been too soft-hearted a few years ago, finds Professional Adjustment and Insurance hogging most of the market south of the river. Attempts to remove the fingernails from prominent PAIN executives have been successful but have provoked a firm response. The FEAR Number Two has been found in a sorry state of disrepair outside the lobby of headquarters. A quick head count suggests that FEAR could possibly conquer PAIN. It would, however, be a close-run thing and could easily go the other way. In these circumstances normal competition-regulation policy is inappropriate. A long-drawn-out war would help nobody except the cops and the handful of punk operators waiting in the wings. A market-sharing agreement, however incompatible with FEAR philosophy, is inevitable.

Cartels are not the end of the world. They are far better than full-blooded competition if outright monopoly control cannot be secured by normal methods. FEAR and PAIN can accept the river as a dividing line and agree not to trespass on each other's territory. The deal will have to be very clear-cut, since no one will be qualified to arbitrate in the case of a dispute. What is required is a self-policing agreement that will be able to handle the fact that each would love to beat the insides out of the other if it could get away with it. Heaven is to attack the opposition and meet no response. Hell is to be attacked and not fight back. A peaceful stand-off, in which no one attacks, is better than all-out war (see figure, p.127).

This is a confrontation very similar to the one that sent Jack the Lad to jail for eight years. There is one important difference. FEAR and PAIN expect to be in business for a very long time. They'll be playing this game over and over again. At first sight, it looks as though each must attack the other, since each does better attacking, whatever the other does. Jack the Lad got out of trouble by joining the Mob, but FEAR and PAIN *are* the Mob. Who can they join? Both sides feel that they have to attack, but each is worse off with an all-

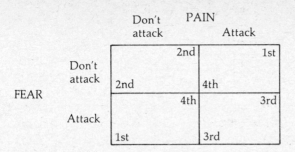

		PAIN	
		Don't attack	Attack
FEAR	Don't attack	2nd 2nd	1st 4th
	Attack	4th 1st	3rd 3rd

FEAR and PAIN feel the need for a cartel

out war. If they could trust each other, they could agree to hold off, but they can't. The way out is to make a *conditional* agreement that takes the form: 'We won't attack if you don't. As soon as you do, the deal is off. We fight back. Nobody wants that.' The agreement is self-policing because each side can unilaterally make it work. It doesn't work for Jack and Flash Harry because once one side talks, it's too late to respond. If PAIN got hold of a neutron bomb that could wipe out the entire FEAR implementation division at a stroke, self-policing would look fragile in this case too. It is crucial, therefore, for each side to retain a substantial second-strike capability. That way any aggressive move for either side plunges the entire informal market into full-scale war.

The consequence of this conditional deal is an uneasy truce. Neither side attacks first, and therefore neither side attacks. One false move destroys the whole thing. Both FEAR and PAIN continue to make money in their respective territories, but each is ready for a massive response to any encroachment by the other. Everyone lives uneasily, but profitably, ever after. The result is nothing like as good for either as having a total monopoly. But it is a lot better than competition.

The ring

Carving up the market into territories will work for existing activities, but it won't solve the problem of what to do when new areas for commercial exploitation emerge. If exciting new business prospects open up outside the allotted territories of the big guns in the market, some method will have to be found of deciding who is going to take advantage of them. One important technique that is available is the ancient technique of the auction ring, a non-violent method of competition regulation much loved by antique dealers.

The principle is simple. First, find an auction. Regular bidders get together and agree not to compete in what most people think of as the *real* auction. A representative of the ring buys all of the interesting merchandise at the lowest possible price. Wasteful competitive bidding between ring members is thus avoided. Of course, others who are not among the ranks of the initiated may spoil things by bidding prices up in an irresponsible and expensive manner. They must be dealt with under the provisions of normal competition policy. Afterwards members of the ring hold a second, *private*, auction. This reflects the prices that they are *really* prepared to pay. Since these prices are considerably higher than those paid by the ring in the first place, the second auction makes a handsome profit. This is shared among ring members according to some agreed formula. (This might result in equal shares or shares in proportion to each member's purchases.) A ring is basically a method for keeping any spare cash in the family rather than handing it over, quite needlessly, to sellers who probably wouldn't know what to do with it anyway.

Perhaps FEAR and PAIN both want the action from a new airport. This is going to be sited, outside the territory of either, in a no-man's-land inhabited by a few small-time operators who can easily be eliminated. The owner will sell the site for 5 million, since he has not had the opportunity to read the confidential report that gives the airport's location. FEAR and PAIN, who *have* seen this report, are both prepared to pay about ten times this figure. If they bid against each other, however, they will end up handing out a small fortune to some degenerate farmer who doesn't deserve it.

They ring the deal and buy for 5 million, assuming that
public relations considerations prevent them from leaning too
hard on the farmer. Now they hold the real auction. As it
happens, neither of the traditional techniques used by rings
to divide up profits works in the complete absence of trust. If
they have a regular private auction and split the profits
equally, PAIN can sucker a lot of money out of FEAR
without ever having any intention of buying the site. FEAR
bids up to 90 million. The ring makes 85 million 'profit'. Split
two ways, that's 42.5 million each. Net cost to FEAR 47.5
million, plus its 2.5 million share of the ring bid. In other
words, FEAR pays the 50 million it would have been
prepared to shell out in a straight showdown in the open
market with no ring. PAIN takes all the real ring profit,
which adds up to 40 million. There's no incentive for FEAR to
join in the first place.

Splitting the ring profits in proportion to the amount that
each party spends has no real meaning when only one item is
on offer. The only reasonably secure method for holding a
ring auction is to use sealed bids and to divide the ring's profit
in proportion to the size of the bids. This way neither side can
exploit the other with any security. A strategic underbid cuts
into your share of the ring profit, while an overbid creates
more ring profit, at your expense, to be shared between the
others.

Ringing a deal is a subtle way of paying competitors not to
bid against you. Your competitors can thereby make money
for doing nothing, so you need to be sure that they are real
competitors, not just a bunch of wide boys who have come
along for the ride. If one particular outfit always seems to get
paid off for just falling short of the highest bid, then it will
have to be dealt with.

SUMMARIZING THE PRINCIPLES OF THE ECONOMICS OF FEAR

The economics of fear depend upon three key principles. The
first of these is the need for an enforcement capability
independent of a state system that not only is cumbersome

and inefficient but also abandons whole areas of the market. Private enforcement agencies can guarantee contracts and will develop implementation divisions that will have many other uses. Those areas of market activity that are abandoned by the state enforcement monopoly will tend to be the most lucrative, for obvious reasons. There will, therefore, be a high demand for contract enforcement in these areas and, consequently, high profits for enforcement agencies.

The second principle concerns the price mechanism. The only system of setting prices that can guarantee maximum profits is to charge consumers the very highest price they are willing to pay for a given product. Any other system, by definition, wastes money. A price mechanism based on competition will inevitably waste money in this way, since competition forces prices down below this optimal level. Competition will be most damaging in those product areas where there is a wide gap between what a consumer is prepared to pay and the price for which a producer can profitably produce the product. Competition will tend to force prices down towards the production cost, with serious losses of potential monopoly profits. Competition, on the other hand, will be relatively harmless when consumers are only prepared to pay a little over the cost of production.

The scope for an active competition policy thus depends upon the product area. When consumers have a physical or psychic addiction to a particular product, an active competition policy will realize enormous monopoly profits. This is when the cost/price gap can be set at its widest. Many of these markets, like sex and drugs, are obvious. Some, such as spare parts for cars, are not and have yet to be fully exploited by competition-regulation agencies. If you need a Volkswagen door, you need a Volkswagen door. Nothing else will fit. So why let customers buy one for next-to-nothing? There are doubtless many other product areas in the straight market that could be developed in this way. All are susceptible to active competition policy.

Provided that competitors can either be directly eliminated or, at the very least, colluded with, monopoly profits should be ensured. All other methods, even killer pricing, waste resources.

The third principle of the economics of fear is the key to the whole thing. It is fear. Traditional economics has failed to realize the extent to which fear is a commodity like any other, with a value that can be traded in for hard cash. The early stages of an active competition policy, for example, will involve a considerable quantity of pain and death. These remedies are expensive to administer. The fear of pain and death is just as effective a deterrent to competition as the real thing. The model that represents the economics of fear is straightforward:

$$f + p + d = m$$

(where f = fear, p = pain, d = death, m = monopoly profit). Even the most superficial inspection of the equation shows that, for a given level of monopoly profit, an increase in the level of (cheap) fear reduces the need for (expensive) pain and death. The level of general welfare in the system is thus increased by fear as a side-effect of the maximization of monopoly profit. (This depends upon the assumption that pain and death are regarded as undesirable.)

Taking a more pessimistic view of the human condition, and assuming the level of pain and death to be constant, k, ($p + d = k$), the cash value of fear can be made even more apparent. An increase in the level of fear increases the level of monopoly profits. The level of potential fear that can conceivably be instilled is bounded only by infinity, but our equation is subject to certain limits. One of these is the total wealth of the world, w. Others are currently being investigated. Fear is thus the key. And to instil fear, you have to develop a reputation for omnipotence. This is the point of the pain and death in the early stages. Once a terrifying reputation has been established, however, the economics of fear will be distinguishable from the economics of anything else only by its higher profit margins.

6

Hijack

The international air piracy business is definitely in decline. There's hardly been a good hijacking in years; yet things looked so hopeful when it all started. Piracy on the high seas, of course, is an ancient and honourable profession. Even Clark Gable made a go of it. Piracy in mid-air has the added advantage that people get pretty jumpy 25,000 feet up in the sky and are inclined to throw all their hard-headed business sense out of the window. More important than this is the fact that airlines are usually super-rich corporations that, as a matter of routine, fork out huge sums of money on supersonic airplanes and other fripperies. They have no call to bat an eyelid at the sorts of sums that would enable a common-or-garden hijacker to enjoy a very sweet old age. Better even than this, modern news media just love a hijacking, a life-and-death drama of epic proportions, packed with real people, weeping relatives and tense big-shots. Each one is a drama that can be guaranteed to unfold at a sparkling pace, have few boring interludes and be topped off with an apocalyptic climax of some sort. This is the sort of thing people pay good money to make films about, yet each hijack is a free show.

From our point of view, the most important thing is that air pirates bargain with their victims. Old-fashioned sea piracy depended too much on the luck of the draw. An enormous quantity of energy had to be expended sailing around looking for a victim, teeming on board and taking over the ship and then sailing around some more. And all that energy might land you nothing more than a boatload of ship's biscuits. Hijackers have the advantage that they can ransom their hostages to a victim who may well be prepared to pay much more for the passengers than for the plane itself. In this sense, hijacking is not piracy at all. It's more like a souped-up version of kidnapping.

The *big* difference is that hijackers are usually surrounded by the angels of justice. This is a positive difference between kidnap and hijack, since hijackers not only have to bargain their payoff out of the victim but they also have to bargain their own way out of a siege. They put their life-style and liberty on the line the moment they stage the takeover. No kidnapper in his right mind puts himself in such a position. Indeed, it is a great comfort to a kidnapper to be holed up in some secret hide-out where no one can get at either him or the hostage. Not only can a kidnapper sit and wait, not only can he unfold the plot at his leisure, but he doesn't have to mess around dealing with the *counter-threats* that add a completely new dimension to the enterprise of hijacking. Since no one knows where a kidnapper is, no one can threaten him. People threaten hijackers all the time, and the added nuisance of having to sort out the boring threats from the interesting ones puts on extra pressure. A hijack, of its essence, is a very public affair. It cannot be negotiated at arm's length and involves the operator in close-quarters confrontation at each stage.

The most common form of hijacking is political. The most common type of hijack demand involves a mixture of cash and concessions, like the release of a bunch of like-minded comrades who have been incarcerated in some far-away jail for doing something that the hijacker doesn't think was that bad. Political hijacking, by definition, puts governments in the role of victim. Hijackings aimed simply at boosting the old bank balance are rather rare. The reasons for this should become obvious.

MOGADISHU: THE STORY

The Mogadishu hijack was a follow-up to the kidnapping of the German industrialist Hans Meyer Schleyer. Both were designed to secure the release from jail of key members of the

Red Army Faction (RAF), an organization that had, in the past, failed to see eye-to-eye with the German government on a number of matters. The best-known of the RAF prisoners were Andreas Baader and Ulrike Meinhof. The hijacking was carried out by Wabil Harb, Hind Alameh, Suhaila Sayeh and Zohair Youssif Akache, four commandos from the Special Operations Division of the Popular Front for the Liberation of Palestine.

On 13 October 1977 Lufthansa flight LH181 was taken over *en route* from Majorca to Frankfurt. It was carrying eighty-six passengers and five crew members. Akache went into the cockpit and stuck a pistol in the pilot's face. He seized the intercom: 'This is Captain Martyr Mahmud speaking. The plane is under my command. Whoever does not follow my instructions will be shot immediately.' The other commandos stood in the cabin holding a grenade in each hand. The pins had been pulled out and dangled from their little fingers.

They wanted to go to Cyprus, but there wasn't enough fuel. Instead they landed in Rome and were quickly encircled by armoured cars. Captain Mahmud relayed his demands over the plane's radio. From a long speech in English the Italians discerned the following demand: 'The group I represent demands the release of our comrades held in German prisons. We are fighting against the world's imperialist organizations.' This message was relayed to the German Minister of the Interior, whose initial reaction was to ask the Italians to shoot out the plane's tyres. The Italian Interior Minister, in consultation with the leader of the Italian Communist Party, decided to get the plane out of Italy as soon as possible. A shoot-out with radical Palestinians on Italian soil would have created internal divisions within the Communist Party, which was giving some support to the government at the time. To have shot out the plane's tyres would have left the hijackers with no alternative but to act out the whole drama at Rome's Fiumicino Airport. The tyres were left alone.

Mahmud demanded fuel and a weather report for Cyprus.

He got both. He requested clearance for take-off. The Italians stalled. He took off anyway. At the same time, the German Inner Cabinet was meeting. It was decided that, whatever happened, the RAF prisoners would not be released.

LH181 landed in Cyprus, and the plane was refuelled. The hijackers prepared to take off for Beirut but were told that Beirut airport had been closed and the runways blocked. They took off for Beirut anyway. The airport was closed, and the runways were blocked. They flew on to Damascus, which was also blocked. They flew on to Baghdad and Kuwait, but both were blocked. (All of this was because the Lufthansa pilot had set a device, fitted to most passenger planes, that identified the plane to ground radar as having been hijacked.)

By now LH181 was nearly out of fuel. The hijackers tried Bahrain but were told that it was blocked. When they arrived, however, the English air traffic controller gave them a hint that one runway was open (he told them the frequency they needed to make an automatic landing). They made a normal landing on an unblocked runway. The plane was surrounded by soldiers. Mahmud put a gun to the pilot's head and threatened to shoot him in five minutes if the soldiers weren't withdrawn. With thirty seconds to go, the soldiers were pulled back. The plane was refuelled and took off for Dubai.

The hijackers' demands had now been clarified. They wanted the release of the RAF prisoners, two Palestinians held in Turkey and $15 million. The deadline was set at 9.00 a.m. on Sunday, 16 October. Back in Germany, the GSG9 anti-terrorist unit was told to prepare to storm the plane.

When LH181 arrived at Dubai, the runways were blocked. After circling for a while, they announced that they were coming in to land. As they made their approach, the fire engines blocking the runway were pulled back and the plane made a normal landing. The plane sat on the tarmac for a day and a night, and nothing much happened.

Captain Mahmud demanded that the plane be refuelled. He set a deadline and threatened to shoot hostages at five-minute intervals after this until the fuel arrived. With seven minutes to go, the fuel arrived. At this stage the deadline for the release of the prisoners was one hour away. The plane took off for Oman. Oman airport, of course, was blocked. They changed course for Aden. When they arrived, they were told it was blocked. They had no more fuel. Flying low over the airport they saw all the runways indeed blocked. They announced that they absolutely had to come down but got no reply. They decided to crash-land on the sand between two runways.

They landed safely, without damaging the plane, and were immediately surrounded by the army. They were told that they had to leave immediately. The airplane's captain, Captain Schumann, was allowed by the hijackers to leave the plane so that he could check the undercarriage for damage. He left but didn't return. Mahmud threatened to blow up the plane if the local soldiers didn't return him. They returned him. Mahmud shot Schumann in the face, and he died instantly. They were once more ordered out of Aden, and the co-pilot eventually managed to take off. From Aden they flew to Mogadishu.

This time they didn't contact the control tower. Mahmud kept watch for planes taking off or landing, and LH181 landed to the complete surprise of the airport authorities. Mahmud offered the co-pilot the chance to leave the plane (leaving no one on board who could fly it), but he wouldn't go.

The German Chargé d'Affaires eventually contacted Mahmud on the radio. Mahmud announced:
'I'm not going to negotiate any more. Our decision is firm. We will blow up the aircraft at 4.00 p. m. with everyone in it if our comrades are not here by then.' Plastic explosive was positioned in the plane; spirit and perfume bottles were emptied on the carpet. Ten minutes before the deadline, Mahmud ordered the Somali soldiers surrounding the plane to withdraw, so that they would not be injured in the explosion. The control tower agreed to pull the soldiers back. Three minutes before the deadline, the Somali Transport

Minister said that he needed more time to communicate the order to all of the soldiers involved. Mahmud gave him another half-hour.

Shortly after this, the German representatives told Mahmud that the government had agreed to release the RAF prisoners. They told him that the prisoners were already on their way to Frankfurt airport. After calculating flying times, Mahmud gave them ten more hours. The Germans, to Mahmud's surprise, accepted the new deadline.

With six hours to go, the German GSG9 commando unit landed at Mogadishu. The RAF prisoners were still in their cells. Twenty-three minutes before the final deadline, the German commandos stormed the plane, killing three out of four hijackers and badly wounding the fourth. No hostages were killed. It was all over in five minutes.

HIJACK VICTIMS

The Mogadishu hijacking was, of course, a failure. It is worth looking at it in some detail, however, to discover whether it could ever have been made to succeed.

The selection of a victim is the first decision made by any hijacker. This is a much more complex procedure than selecting a kidnap victim, mainly because it is never quite clear who a hijack victim is. In one sense the problem is quite simple. The victim is the person or organization that the hijackers want to pressurize into making concessions. For a political hijacker, therefore, there are usually a few obvious victims and almost always one prime victim. With the Mogadishu hijack the most obvious victim was the German government, since only it could agree to release the RAF prisoners.

The situation was rather complicated, however, by the hijack demand for the release of two prisoners in Turkish jails. The fact that no Turkish hostages were taken, while the aircraft belonged to the German state airline, meant that the only hope of freeing the prisoners in Turkey lay in pressure exerted on Turkey by the German government. This meant that even with respect to the prisoners in foreign jails, the Germans were the victims.

The point about both kidnap and hijack is that the hostage and the victim must be related. If they are not, the threat to kill the hostage cuts no ice. This is a great imponderable with any hijacking, since it is almost impossible to know in advance which particular collection of passports will be in the passenger compartment when the plane is taken. There will be a collection of secondary victims in any hijacking, the most obvious of which are those governments whose citizens are among the hostages. Many of these governments will not be facing demands from the hijackers. This means that they cannot directly influence the course of events. Notwithstanding this, they may be able to bring varying amounts of pressure to bear upon the direct victim in order to protect their own interests. Sometimes, of course, a powerful government can force a weak government to do more or less whatever it wants. Then the relationship between the victims is obviously crucial. If the direct victim is a powerful government, the other victims may well be irrelevant. If the direct victim is a weak government, particularly if it is heavily dependent on one of the secondary victims, the situation can be very complex. Obviously, if there is a group of direct victims, the problem of getting them all to dance to the same tune may be insuperable.

As a hijacker, the most obvious way of simplifying these matters is to concentrate on the state-run airline of the main victim. This at least increases the chance that a fair number of the hostages will be of the victim's nationality. Air travel being a cosmopolitan business, it is impossible to guarantee that *only* victim nationals will be bagged. The hijacker obviously retains the option, if he wants to simplify matters, of releasing all non-victim nationals in the group of hostages. (Such simplification may not help the hijacker. At Entebbe, after the hijackers had released all non-Israeli hostages, it became much easier for the Israelis to launch their successful rescue mission.) At Mogadishu the airplane was German, the hostages were mainly German and the principal victim was the German government. That, at least, was straightforward.

Another secondary victim in a hijacking is the government on whose soil the final act of the drama is played out. There is really very little to be gained, and an awful lot to be lost, in having a hijacked airliner land at your airport. If the hijackers blow up the plane, or if a rescue mission fails, the 'host' government will take a lot of the blame. Life is made much simpler if the hijacked airliner is denied the chance to land. Thus, between 13 October and 18 October 1977, the authorities at Beirut, Damascus, Baghdad, Kuwait, Dubai, Oman and Aden airports all refused to allow LH181 to land. At Dubai and Aden, this was despite the fact that they had been told that the plane would crash if it did not land. The authorities at Rome and Cyprus, although they allowed the plane to land, wanted the plane off their land as soon as possible. The Somalis had no choice because the hijackers landed without warning air traffic control. No one welcomed LH181 with open arms.

THE THREATS

When a hijacked airliner is circling your airport requesting landing permission, you have quite a tough decision to make, complicated by the fact that you won't be able to believe anything the hijackers say. Your desires and theirs will often be in direct conflict. Viewed from the ground, there are three possibilities. If you agree to allow the plane to land, it will do so, presumably undamaged, and will thus be able to take off again. There is some chance that the climax of the hijacking will occur on your soil, but a good chance that it will move off elsewhere. However, once the plane is down, you can't force it to take off again, and you are not left with a very effective arsenal of threats to bring to bear on the hijacker. 'If the plane doesn't take off in ten minutes, we'll. . . .' You'll *what*? Have a tantrum? Open fire on the plane? You can cut off ground power and refuse food if you want to bring pressure to bear, but when the chips are down, you will not risk the lives of the hostages by rejecting an ultimatum demanding that these be restored.

If you refuse permission, presumably because you don't believe them when they say that they haven't enough fuel to go anywhere else, two things might happen. Either they will crash-land anyway (because they really don't have any fuel left) or they will go elsewhere (because they do). *You* will never know whether they have the fuel or not. *They* will often not know for certain whether they can make the next airport. Maybe they have just enough fuel, but the winds are bad. Maybe the engines have been damaged and the fuel consumption can't be accurately estimated. The hijackers may face a choice between a certain crash-landing at your airport or a risky flight to the next (which may anyway be blocked and leave them with the same problem). Once all the airports are blocked, the odds will be heavily in favour of their making a crash-landing, regardless of the blocked runways.

If the plane makes a crash-landing, that is the worst thing that can happen to you. If the landing is unsuccessful and everyone is killed, the outcome is worse than having the hijackers blow up the plane at your airport. Your refusal to grant landing permission is the direct cause of the crash, and you bear the responsibility. If the plane crash-lands and badly damages itself, it will not be able to take off again. You will have guaranteed that a major episode, if not the final act, of the drama will be acted out on your soil. The best that you can hope for then is to give the hijackers another plane straightaway and pack them off — but transfers of this sort are risky. Only if the plane crash-lands with no damage (the result at Aden) are you in as good a position as if you had given landing permission in the first place.

Given all of this, the most sensible course of action would seem to be to refuse landing permission when it is requested, to block the runways in case they come to take a look, but to block them in such a way that they can be unblocked quickly if the hijacked airliner seems to have committed itself to making a landing. This is what Dubai did and what Aden did not do. The authorities at Aden were very lucky. Obviously, there is nothing to lose by refusing permission in the first place. It may discourage the hijackers from wasting fuel by coming to take a look.

From the point of view of the hijacker, bargaining leverage is most limited while the plane is in the air. He can always threaten to kill a hostage for every five minutes for which landing permission is refused, but there will be no way that the ground authorities can discover whether or not the threat is being carried out. Hijackings cause peculiar communication problems. We shall see later that these can be put to good use by hijackers. Sometimes, however, these problems weaken the bargaining position of hijackers. A threat to kill hostages will obviously be more effective if it can be enacted for all to see and should be saved for such occasions. Thus an airborne hijacker looking at an empty fuel gauge and a blocked runway is in the unenviable position of having no alternative course of action but to trust in the rationality of the ground authorities. The blocked runway *should* be cleared at the last minute if the ground authorities are thinking straight, but no one likes to expose himself to that sort of risk.

The Mogadishu hijacking involved a number of threats to kill the hostages, each made for different reasons. There was the main threat, directed against the German government, to kill the hostages if the RAF prisoners were not released by 9.00 a.m. on Sunday, 16 October. There was the threat in Bahrain to kill the pilot in five minutes if soldiers surrounding the plane were not withdrawn. This was directed against the Bahrain army commander and was acceded to. There was the threat at Dubai to shoot hostages at five-minute intervals if the plane was not refuelled. This was directed against the Dubai authorities and was successful. There was the threat in Aden to blow up the plane unless the missing pilot was returned for execution. This was directed against the military commander at Aden and was acceded to. Schumann was executed.

Each of the threats against subsidiary victims was successful. In each case, presumably, the decision to give in was made on the grounds that the stakes were too high to risk hostages' lives. In each case the deadlines were very short, and spot decisions had to be made. In each case it was clear that the hijackers would have found it hard to back down without losing all credibility and effectively abandoning the hijacking. Most important, in each case, bowing to the hijackers' threats cost the secondary victims, in Bahrain, Dubai and Aden, very little.

The main threat, made against the central victim, is, of course, the crux of any hijacking. In order to analyse this, we must first decide whether the hijackers mean what they say.

The posthumous payoff

There are a number of very important differences between the threats made by hijackers and those made by kidnappers, blackmailers or extortionists. The most spectacular difference is obviously the fact that hijackers often make threats that involve killing themselves along with the hostages. Anyone who takes a plane complete with passengers and threatens to blow it up if certain demands are not met is in a very different bargaining position from a colleague who places a remote-control bomb on the same plane and makes the same demands from the safety of a well concealed mountain hideaway. The remote threat is really a rather clever variation on the old protection game. The threat to blow yourself up along with all of the passengers adds a completely new dimension to the problems facing the victim.

When discussing the best methods of threatening people, I made it clear that real threats involve the possibility that if the threat is called, the threatener will have to do something that he would much rather avoid. The only really juicy threats are the ones you hope you won't have to carry out. In these terms, the hijack threat is the granddaddy of all real threats. Given the special significance that many people attach to death, however, it makes sense to talk separately about real threats that involve the threatener's suicide. For one thing, the reason why people carry out threats that harm themselves is so that others will take them more seriously in the future. Real threats are enacted to enhance credibility.

But when I threaten to kill myself if you don't give me £5, and if you actually care whether I live or die, blowing out my own brains when you fail to deliver will not get me very far. It will, of course, enhance my credibility. You will know that I meant what I said. I, however, will have no further use for this credibility, although it would be appropriate for you to have some fitting epitaph inscribed upon the headstone of my grave.

There is another side to this. Some people would like to go out in a blaze of glory. If you've got to go anyway, you might as well do it in style. Those who either suffer from terminal diseases or have decided for other reasons that life isn't worth living can be very tough opponents when it comes to making threats (as we saw, in another context, in chapter 2). They're tough because they need a pretext to go out in style. There is, however, a paradox that should discourage such people from involving themselves too deeply in the threatening business. Since they are such a tough proposition, the victim will probably capitulate. *If* the victim capitulates, the threatener loses the chance to carry out the threat and go out in a blaze of glory. The whole purpose is self-defeating. This suggests that suicidal operators should not involve themselves in threatening on a mercenary basis — unless, of course, lack of money is the cause of the original suicidal tendency. When this is the case, the suicidal threatener is almost unbeatable. He should, of course, be employed on the basis of a percentage of the net profit from the threat if it is successful. Such people, however, may be rare.

A much tougher proposition is the opponent who doesn't actively want to die but who sees benefits from his actions continuing to accumulate after death. For cynical atheists this is inconceivable. All payoffs stop at the point of death, and posthumous income is irrelevant. Cynical atheists should not indulge in hijacking unless they can successfully conceal this serious bargaining liability. Anyone who spotted a cynical atheist for what he really was would laugh in his face when he threatened to commit suicide (the only exception being the cynical atheist who is also tired of life and is prepared to sacrifice all for a few seconds of exquisite satisfaction). On the other hand, those who believe in something more than themselves will, in certain circumstances, regard dying as not the very worst thing that can happen to them. Those who believe in life after death see the payoffs continuing on into the next world, even after they vacate this one. Idealists and religious believers may, therefore, go into the hijacking business plausibly, since their suicide threats must be taken seriously. In each case, since there is at least a possibility of achieving a payoff after death, the hijack threat is credible.

What might such posthumous payoffs comprise? The believer in life after death could conceivably think that his credibility will go with him to the next world. Thus, by carrying out a hijack threat on Earth, he will be better equipped to threaten people in Heaven. This produces a strong incentive to carry out suicidal threats but seems inconsistent with most views of Heaven put forward by the religious authorities. Those who believe in Heaven see it as a pleasant place, where there is no room for hijacking, blackmail, extortion, kidnapping and other professions that critically depend on credible threats. Indeed, few views of Heaven put forward by those in the know even mention threats as a significant element in posthumous existence. This means that posthumous payoffs must be denominated in currencies other than fear. For example, many religious types believe that they will be rewarded in Heaven for worthy deeds on Earth.

Many religions can easily accommodate the notion of the Just War and hence the notion of Just Killing. The notion of Just Killing opens the way for Just Hijacking. The Just Hijacker would believe that the explosion that killed himself and the hostages would Do Good in the long run; it would be an earthly act that would be rewarded in Heaven, the immediate destination of the perpetrator. A forward-looking sort of religious fanatic would thus be prepared to put up with some inconvenience in the short term in exchange for a handsome posthumous dividend.

Such people make formidable hijackers, whose threats

must be taken seriously. Since they are not suicidal, they will be prepared to bargain. The Good Deed may be effectively achieved by sparing the hostages in exchange for the concessions demanded. Indeed, killing the hostages unnecessarily might well be seen as a reprehensible act by whoever is in charge of the Celestial Kitty and punished in the hereafter. On the other hand, if the concessions are not forthcoming, then killing the hostages will generally enhance the credibility of the Just Hijacking movement, advance the aims of the deity in question and hence be worthy of reward.

It is occasionally argued that some people other than religious fanatics are also unconcerned with maximizing their own well being. There is a very simple argument against this, which goes as follows: 'If such people do something that makes them worse off but benefits others, they must do it for a reason. They must have a desire to do it, and fulfilling this desire must satisfy them. Even if being a goody-goody makes them miserable, they must want to do whatever makes them miserable. They must, therefore, enjoy being miserable, which is merely another form of self-centred enjoyment. There is no such thing as an altruist, only a masochist.' (Anyone who is interested in pursuing this matter in greater depth should take up philosophy.) Attractive as the argument is, it is an indisputable fact that there are some philosophers who regard it as a load of bourgeois rubbish. For their benefit, I will allow a few altruists into the world of hijacking. This is actually quite convenient, since altruists make excellent hijackers.

An altruist is someone who is not solely concerned with his own payoffs. It is clear that some altruists, like Captain Martyr Mahmud, will be prepared to die for others. Balancing the considerable disadvantages of being blown up in a Boeing 737 against the advancement of some altruistic cause, such as the liberation of Palestine, the bottom line may indicate a kamikaze mission. Not only will the cause be brought to the attention of that relatively small proportion of the world's population with access to the mass media, but future victims will also take note of the fact that Altruistic

Hijackers mean business. The next one may be taken seriously and the cause consequently furthered. Only twenty-seven people outside Holland and South Molucca knew anything at all about the problems facing the South Moluccan people until they hijacked a train. The hijackers changed that overnight, even if they didn't get what they wanted.

While the Altruist would be prepared to die if the price was right, he would rather not if the concessions were granted. He develops the same concern for credibility as the professional kidnapper or the Just Hijacker. The sudden termination of his life, even if he does not believe in Heaven, is no problem. His enhanced credibility can be bequeathed to his comrades. Such people are not masochists; they are willing martyrs.

To summarize: the critical thing one needs to know about any hijacker is his or her attitude to death. The hijacker who is not prepared to die, and who is known to think like this, is doomed to failure. Exclusively selfish motivations, those of Atheists, produce:

		Selfish Atheistic Hijacker	
		No blow	Blow
Victim	Pay	1st	4th
	No pay	2nd	4th

A Selfish Atheist plays at hijacking

Since there are no circumstances in which such a person is going to blow up the plane, his threats can be safely ignored. A consequence of this is that the hijacked plane should never be stormed by the anti-terrorist industry. There is nothing to be gained and lives could conceivably be lost. (I will return to the decision to storm hijacked airliners later.)

The Suicidal Hijacker is the polar opposite of the Selfish one:

Suicidal Hijacker

		No blow	Blow
Victim	Pay	4th	2nd
	No pay	4th	1st

The morbid view of a Suicidal Hijacker

We can assume that the Suicidal Hijacker's blaze of glory is somewhat dampened if the plane is blown up after the demands have been met. Nevertheless, the Suicidal Hijacker is impossible to bargain with. Since he is going to blow the plane up regardless, there is no incentive to pay.

The Just Hijacker and the Altruist amount to one and the same three people for these purposes. The Three Just Hijackers want most of all not to have to make martyrs of themselves and for the victim to give in (pay/no blow comes top of the list). Like all professionals, Just Hijacker Mark I and Just Hijacker Mark II are overwhelmingly concerned with the credibility of their operation. To safeguard the good name of future Just Acts, they must carry out the threat if their demands are not heeded (no pay/blow comes second). Mark I and Mark II differ only over their responses to failure. Mark I feels that it is better to win the concession and kill the hostages anyway than it is to get nothing and spare them — pay/blow. The Just Concession outweighs the lives of the hostages. Mark II feels that killing hostages when the concession has been granted is very bad publicity for Just Causes in general, since it will be widely regarded as an unJust thing to do. Mark II would rather lose everything, including the demand and all credibility. Mark III is a hijacker who regards the concession as all-important.

Gaining the concession dwarfs any concern for future credibility, although if the cause wins anyway, it is better to spare the hostages (pay/no blow is top of the list, closely followed by pay/blow). If the concession is not forced out of the victim, credibility can be salvaged by killing the hostages, so that no pay/blow beats no pay/no blow. This last is the very worst thing that can happen to a Mark III.

Just Hijacker Mark I

	No blow	Blow
Pay	1st	3rd
No pay	4th	2nd

Victim

Just Hijacker Mark II

	No blow	Blow
Pay	1st	4th
No pay	3rd	2nd

Victim

Just Hijacker Mark III

	No blow	Blow
Pay	1st	2nd
No pay	4th	3rd

Victim

The Three Just Hijackers

I will not trespass on the jurisdiction of philosophers and theologians by choosing between the three different ways of viewing the mind of a Just Hijacker. As a matter of fact, this is not even necessary. For the purposes of this argument, they all share one common property: the Three Just Hijackers would each rather not blow up the plane if the victim pays and would each rather blow up the plane if the victim does not. This means we have some real action on our hands.

Captain Martyr Mahmud did not choose his alias casually. He and his colleagues were, quite precisely, martyrs and must have had the preferences of a Just Hijacker. It is clear that they were prepared to die, and my guess is that they had a Mark II view of the world. They developed friendly relations with some of the hostages, while still wanting above all for the RAF prisoners to be released. This means that they felt that the best thing that could happen was for the prisoners *and* the hostages to be released. They must have thought that the worst thing that could have happened was for the hostages to die needlessly. If the RAF prisoners were not released, however, and the hijackers' demands were rejected, the cause for which they were fighting was sufficiently important to them to kill the hostages in order to retain its credibility.

TO PAY OR NOT TO PAY?

Almost without exception, hijack victims are professionals. At the very least, they tend to be the governments of small or medium-sized countries, but they may well be large and wealthy corporations or even super-powers. All victims, therefore, have some concern for credibility. They know that to give in once is to increase future vulnerability. Yet hijackings are spectacular events, and media coverage is intense. Huge pressure builds up on those making the decisions to forget about the long-term benefits of taking a hard line.

The victim's dilemma is complicated by the fact that most of the long-term benefits of a tough no-pay policy are shared among all potential victims, while all of the costs of such a policy are paid by the victim of the day. If I run a smallish country, I may feel that discouraging hijackers in general is a good thing. I know that storming airplanes and slaughtering hijackers does discourage the others, but *which* others will be discouraged? Most of these other hijackers will be operating half-way around the world. Why should I pay for an easier ride for other governments with the lives of my loyal subjects? Some of the incentives to hang tough will be diluted by the fact that the benefits are general, while the costs are quite specific. The chances that a pro victim will behave like an amateur are increased. On the other hand, hijackings are public affairs, and the prospects of keeping them quiet are slim. One incentive to act like an amateur is removed, since there's no chance of giving in on the quiet.

The victim may then feel one of these two ways about the hijacking:

The reaction of Victims A and B

Victim A thinks like a pro and would be prepared to sacrifice the hostages to maintain credibility. First choice for both victims is no pay/no blow; last choice for both is pay/blow. Victims A and B differ because A would rather not pay, building credibility at the cost of dead hostages, while B is overwhelmed by the desire to save the hostages, at any cost, to safeguard future bargaining power.

At heart both victims are pros and both *really* think like Victim A. The pressures of public opinion and the fact that governments rather than hijackers seem to get blamed when hostages get killed can, however, weaken the resolve of the toughest pro. The German government had already suffered a serious setback at the Munich Olympics as a result of taking a tough line and losing hostages. It knew the price it might pay if the passengers on flight LH181 were harmed. In the early stages of the hijacking it hedged its bets. Although a firm decision not to release the RAF prisoners was made at the outset, the pursuit aircraft carrying German negotiators also contained the ransom money.

Since nearly all governments adopt a soft line only under duress, they seize on any pretext to act like pros. One of the rules of the game seems to be that once any hostage is killed, the government can behave as if they were all dead and launch an immediate counter-attack. Thus, while the Germans may have been tempted, with memories of Munich, to act like Victim B in the early stages, once Schumann, the pilot, was shot, there can be little doubt that they saw through the eyes of Victim A.

Once the victim thinks like a pro and is prepared to sacrifice the hostages in the name of credibility, not paying is the overwhelmingly dominant strategy. Victim A simply doesn't pay, whatever type of hijacker he may be confronting. As we can see from the Compleat and Unabridged Game of Just Hijacking, prospects for the hostages look bleak. The Just Hijacker has no dominant strategy, blowing up the plane or not according to the victim's first move. This makes no difference to the victim's thinking. The inevitable outcome, therefore, is no pay/blow.

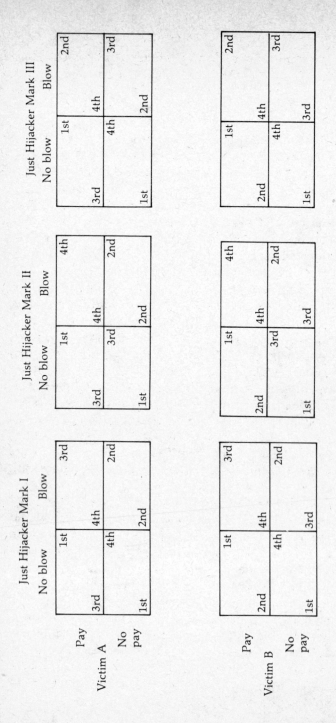

The Compleat and Unabridged Game of Just Hijacking

Each of the Three Just Hijackers prefers to blow the plane up if the victim doesn't pay. If Victim A moves first, the response to the inevitable first move is clear. If the hijacker moves first, or if both move independently, each Just Hijacker must anticipate Victim A's failure to pay. The hostages are bound to die if they are not rescued first.

If the victim is prepared to sacrifice credibility and the safety of potential future hostages in exchange for the lives of the hijacked passengers, the problem is a little more complicated. Victim B still has no pay as a dominant strategy, but the order of moves now makes a difference. If the victim moves first, he does better by *not* playing his dominant strategy and paying up, whichever Just Hijacker he happens to be confronting. If the victim doesn't pay, the Just Hijacker blows up the plane. Victim B prefers pay/no blow to no pay/blow and can guarantee this by paying promptly.

The deadline set by the hijackers is once more an integral part of the problem, since it enables a distinction to be made between the victim who has *not paid yet* and the victim who has actually made the move of *not paying*. Thus Victim B finds himself in the same predicament as a freelance kidnap victim facing a kidnapper who is prepared to kill the hostage. He will rush to pay and to beat the deadline; he is forced to abandon a dominant strategy and co-operate with the hijacker.

The fact that hijackings attract a blaze of publicity means that secret deals are less likely. Thus the pro victim cannot try to pay in private and thus salvage credibility by hushing up the whole thing. This can get a pro kidnap victim off the hook in certain circumstances, and it suggests that hijackers who value their demands more highly than publicity might try to hijack some valuable cargo in secret and deal with the victim on the basis of continued discretion. Airlines with live passengers will not be much good. All those relatives will get curious during the negotiations, and someone will blow the story to the press. Other cargos might, however, do the trick.

Imagine the hijacking of a plane, ship or train carrying valuable and dangerous nuclear fuel. Not only would the cargo be valuable enough to be worth paying a considerable price for, but also the owners would be very embarrassed to admit that such a cargo could be hijacked at all. Such incompetence would give too much ammunition to the anti-nuclear lobby.

The cargo would be missed only by its owners and a few employees who could be bought off or otherwise silenced. The hijacking would become big news only if either side chose to talk to the press, and neither side would have an incentive to do so. A Just Hijacker could now make considerable secret demands, promising not to talk if these were granted. The victim would have a strong incentive to give in, or at the very least, to deal. The costs of public disclosure would be added to those more directly threatened by the nuclear hijacker. The hijacker would have an incentive to keep quiet in order to be able to pull the same stunt again. Once he had talked, no future victim would believe a promise of secrecy. The government *might* pay up, faced with something that comes quite close to the perfect crime. This version of nuclear hijacking combines some of the most potent features of hijacking with some of the pressures that a blackmailer brings to bear on his victim. The public, of course, would never find out. (As a matter of fact, a successful nuclear hijack has been pulled off twice already.)

STORMING THE CITADEL

Recent public hijackings have usually resulted in a full frontal assault on the hijacked airliner. Such assaults have typically ended with the death of the hijackers and the rescue of most of the hostages. Both Mogadishu and Entebbe provided spectacular examples of this particular endgame. Most hijack victims are governments, and many governments now maintain special CRW (Counter-Revolutionary Warfare) units that regularly practise bursting into airplanes and shooting hijackers. The British SAS, the German GSG9 and equivalent units elsewhere have become potent bargaining chips in their own right. Hijackers now know that a victim government can get at them if it really wants to and is prepared to put hostages' lives at risk.

For a victim, sending in the SAS is a decision similar to calling the cops in a kidnapping. With a hijacking, of course, the cops are called straightaway, so that particular decision doesn't have to be taken. The important point of similarity is that once the SAS has been sent in, no more decisions have to be taken. The victim commits himself irrevocably to not paying. This means that a full frontal assault will be attempted only if the victim has decided not to pay anyway. However, having decided not to pay, full frontal assault is not the only possible choice. The alternative is to do nothing.

Governments must therefore decide between sitting on their hands and storming the citadel. Their choice will depend upon the expected result of inaction. We have already seen that a Mercenary Hijacker has no incentive to carry out the threat, while a Suicidal Hijacker has no incentive not to. A Just Hijacker will carry it out if his demands are not granted. A government dealing with a Mercenary Hijacker has no incentive to pay, but he has no incentive to launch a rescue mission either. The hostages will not die, and a rescue mission will merely introduce the chance that they will be shot in error by the rescuers. Total inactivity seems the only sensible response. The hijacker should eventually realize the hopelessness of his position or be bored into submission.

Faced with a Suicidal Hijacker, a full frontal assault is one answer. The hijacker is looking for any pretext to kill the hostages and precipitate his hour of glory. If the government is in any way inclined to press the issue, there's only one way to press it — by attacking. The hijacker is probably going to kill the hostages anyway, and a rescue mission holds out some chance of saving their lives. On the other hand, the Suicidal Hijacker is probably after a glorious exit. After all, there are easier ways of ending it all than hijacking an airliner and blowing yourself up. An alternative government response is to ignore the hijacking completely. This involves *total* inactivity. No ring of troops, no communication, no business as usual. If all possibilities of glory are denied him, the hijacker may decide to get his final thrill at somebody else's expense. The only problem with this strategy is that the victim will be in serious trouble if it goes wrong. It's one thing to lose a planeload of hostages. Most governments don't really mind that too much once the chips are down. It's quite another thing to lose a planeload as a result of a bungle or of negligence. Governments have to be seen to be doing their best for innocent citizens, and sending the hijacker to Coventry, however sensible, can be hard to explain. Nothing looks more like doing your best than sending in the SAS.

Faced with a Just Hijacker, the decision to launch a rescue mission will depend on how the government is feeling. If it has given up on its credibility and has decided to pay, the SAS should be kept busy in another hemisphere. Nothing is to be gained from flash-bang grenades and sharp shooting. If the government has decided that it would rather see the hostages blown away than lose face, then there's going to be some killing anyway. Nothing can be lost by sending in the heavy mob, and lives might even be saved. This seems to be the most common response of recent hijack victims, the Germans and Israelis being notable examples. There is little doubt that the Mogadishu hostages would have been released if the hijackers' demands had been granted. The German government, despite this, decided not to grant the demands. There is little doubt that Captain Mahmud was prepared to kill the hostages if his demands weren't granted. This left the victim with no choice but GSG9.

The decision about whether or not to send in a rescue mission is thus very simple. If a Mercenary Hijacker is involved, you never do it. If a Just Hijacker makes you want to pay, the hard men can't help you. If you're prepared to face it out, the hard men are your only hope. The only tough decision is the one you have to make as you face a Suicidal Hijacker, when the possibility of ignoring him totally may tantalize you.

The main problem is to decide which particular type of hijacker is involved. The Mercenary is easy to spot by his distinctive demands. These are very mercenary. They involve lots of money and little else. The Suicidal Hijacker should be easy to spot by the total impossibility of his demands. No one who wants to go out in a blaze of glory should leave open the possibility of capitulation by the victim. The Just Hijacker will make feasible demands that involve more than money. His demands will be distinctively Just. It's simple really, although two thousand amateur and professional psychologists will be only too happy to advise if you're still in doubt. These days most governments are worried about their image, and most hijackers are Just. That's why most hijackings end in a shoot-out.

7

Siege

Nobody wants to end up in a siege. Hijackers choose to hijack; kidnappers choose to kidnap; blackmailers often quite like blackmailing. Sieges are usually mistakes.

A firm of bank robbers is quietly going about its business, robbing a bank and scaring the customers, when the sirens start wailing and fifty armed policemen surround the premises. There's nothing for it but to grab a customer, insert a sawn-off shotgun into his mouth and tell the forces of justice to mind their own business. Minding their own business is not what the forces of justice are good at. In no time at all, they've got marksmen with high-velocity rifles and night sights swinging from every local lamp post. They settle down for a long wait. Since most policemen find sieges a lot more fun than issuing parking tickets, the bank robbers are in a hole.

At this stage, they are quite happy to leave the money behind them. They wish they'd never even stepped inside the bank in the first place. Most of all, they want to go home, go to bed and forget the whole business, but the cops have other ideas. The cops want them behind bars. Holed up in the bank, the robbers have only one real demand. They want to be free. People stuck in sieges may ask for helicopters, planes and fast cars, but they didn't get up in the morning and decide to take some hostages and to threaten to kill them if they don't get a free ride in a helicopter. When the crunch arrives, the helicopter just seems like a nice safe method of getting out of the way of those night sights.

Whether there is any real action at all in a siege depends on two things. In the first place, it depends on whether the robbers have got one hostage or a roomful of them. In the second place, it depends upon how they feel about going to jail. If there's only one hostage, things can be pretty difficult. After all, once the hostage is killed there's nothing to stop the police from piling in and, at the very best, hauling the killers off to the nearest prison. Knowing this, the cops will be confident that the hostage will be killed only as a last resort. If there is a roomful of hostages, the possibility of shooting them one at a time provides a much better bargaining position.

To complicate things further, there is also the possibility that being picked off by police marksmen may not seem much worse to the besieged robber than half a lifetime spent in some institute of correction. In this case, running a high risk of a bullet in the head may seem worth a slight improvement in the chances of staying out of jail.

Imagine first, however, that the robbers *do* care about getting killed. They would rather spend the next few years in a jail than in a cemetery. Imagine, too, that they have only one hostage. Presumably, they will think like this:

| | | Robbers | |
		Don't kill	Kill
Cops	Give in	1st	2nd
	Stand firm	3rd	4th

Robbers stuck in a siege but otherwise enjoying life and holding one hostage

As far as the robbers are concerned, the best thing that can happen is that the cops give in and let the robbers go free, while the robbers spare the hostage. The worst thing that can happen is the reverse: the cops stand firm, while the robbers kill the hostage. The cops then over-run the robbers and generally give them a hard time. If the cops give in, it is better to spare the hostage than to kill him. Killing the hostage only generates more heat later. Likewise, if the cops stand firm, it's better to spare the hostage. After all, murder only results in a bigger jail sentence than straightforward bank robbery.

The cops don't like giving in. It makes them look stupid. As far as they are concerned, the best thing that can happen is to stand firm and have the robbers spare the hostage. The worst that can happen is to give in and have the hostage killed anyway. After this, it depends on whether the cops are Soft or Tough. A Tough Cop would rather see the hostages dead than the robbers free:

		Robbers	
		Don't kill	Kill
Tough Cop	Give in	3rd	4th
	Stand firm	1st	2nd

A Tough Cop's view of the siege game

A Soft Cop would rather see the hostages alive than the robbers caught:

		Robbers	
		Don't kill	Kill
Soft Cop	Give in	2nd	4th
	Stand firm	1st	3rd

A soft equivalent

As a matter of fact, it doesn't make much difference how Tough (or Soft) the cops are when they deal with a one-hostage siege. The results are the same:

Robbers (one hostage)

		Don't kill	Kill
Soft Cop	Give in	1st 2nd	2nd 4th
	Stand firm	3rd 1st	4th 3rd

		Don't kill	Kill
Tough Cop	Give in	1st 3rd	2nd 4th
	Stand firm	3rd 1st	4th 2nd

The stakes in a one-hostage siege

The robbers have a dominant strategy of not killing. They get their first choice rather than their second if the cops give in, and their third choice rather than their fourth if they don't. Both types of cop have a dominant strategy: stand firm. Since both sides have dominant strategies, regardless of the toughness of the cops, the outcome looks pretty definite. It is difficult to predict anything but stand firm/don't kill. The order of the moves makes no difference, since each side has a choice that is better regardless of the choice of the other. Furthermore, no alternative outcome is preferred by both cops and robbers. This means that there is not much scope for a deal.

Given all of this, a full frontal assault on the siege does not look to be a very sensible strategy for the cops. Standing firm is sufficient to get what they want. The robbers should eventually realize that they're not going to win and give themselves up. This is certainly the line taken on sieges (or 'hostage situations', as they are known to the trade) by the New York Police Department (NYPD). Their policy of total inactivity, combined with intransigence disguised as convincingly as possible as co-operation, has led to a high success rate and few dead hostages.

The position is a little different if the robbers have a bankful or a busload of hostages. In the first place, one or two hostages can be killed by the robbers to make the point that they mean business. Killing the odd hostage also puts the robbers in a very different bargaining position. They are murderers and have nothing to lose by killing again. The cops have very little to offer in order to entice them out. This is complicated by the fact that full-scale frontal assaults tend to be launched by the forces of justice at the killing of the first hostage. We will investigate the logic of this shortly. The fact remains that you might as well hang for two murders as for one. Provided that whoever you are dealing with is concerned to protect the lives of the remaining live hostages, killing one of the bunch can greatly enhance your bargaining position. It does this in the same way as any other form of irrevocable commitment to a given course of action.

Robbers who hold a group of hostages never have any incentive to kill the whole lot at one go. This would put them in the same position as if they had a single hostage and would destroy the bargaining leverage that derives from their ability to kill hostages one at a time. They may *threaten* to kill the whole lot, of course, but this threat will cut no ice at all. The only threat that will cut ice is the threat to kill the hostages one by one. This retains bargaining leverage while enhancing credibility. The decision facing the robbers, therefore, is not whether to kill the hostages but whether to kill the *first* hostage.

The clear possibility now emerges that the robbers will prefer, if the cops stand firm, to kill the first hostage rather than not. While there is no incentive for robbers with only one hostage to destroy their only hope of a few hours of freedom, there is a strong incentive for robbers with a roomful of hostages to execute one to show the world that they mean business. (As a matter of fact, two hostages are no

Robbers

		Don't kill first hostage	Kill first hostage
Cops	Give in	1st	2nd
	Stand firm	4th	3rd

Robbers with a roomful of hostages

better than one in this respect. There is no incentive to kill the first, since this leaves only one live hostage. As we have seen, this is a hopeless position. It might, from this, be argued that *three* hostages are no better than one. The first will never be killed, because this would leave two, and the first of these would never be killed because that would leave one. A pedantic nuisance could go the whole hog and argue, therefore, that it was no better to have *a thousand* hostages than to have one. The first would never be killed, since that would only leave nine hundred and ninety-nine. The first of these would never be killed. . . and so on. This is an example of something that is known to pedantic nuisances as a 'last-game paradox'. With a roomful of hostages at stake, you will need an awful lot of pedantry in your heart to bet their lives against a last-game paradox.)

Apart from the opportunity for the robbers to show that they mean business, the game is unchanged. This possibility, however, drastically influences the likely course of events.

The robbers now have no dominant strategy. They prefer to kill if the cops stand firm, and they prefer not to kill if the cops give in. This means that the order of moves is now critical. If the robbers must make the first move, or must move at the same time as the cops, then they must kill. They have to assume that the cops will play their dominant strategy, stand firm. If this happens, kill/stand firm is the outcome.

		Robbers	
		Don't kill first hostage	Kill first hostage
Soft Cops	Give in	1st 2nd	2nd 4th
	Stand firm	4th 1st	3rd 3rd

		Robbers	
		Don't kill first hostage	Kill first hostage
Tough cops	Give in	1st 3rd	2nd 4th
	Stand firm	4th 1st	3rd 2nd

The options broaden

When the robbers face Tough Cops, this is what will actually take place. The Tough Cops are happy enough with this, their second choice, and there is certainly no alternative that both they and the robbers prefer. A deal is not on the cards, and the Tough Cops have no incentive to make the first move. If they did make the first move, it would be to stand firm. This is the same move as they make if they go second. Kill/stand firm looks to be the unstoppable outcome. In practice, this is why the Tough Cops have an incentive to launch a full frontal assault. There is no reason for them to suppose, after the first round has been played out and a hostage executed, that the same threat won't be made again. There is no reason for them to suppose that there will not be the same outcome, a dead hostage. And so on. If Tough Cops play it this way, the robbers just execute the hostages one by one until they have only one left, at which point the game changes. (Perceptive robbers may spot the last-game paradox as it approaches and stop killing hostages at an earlier point.) Whatever happens, this police strategy results in dead hostages. A full frontal assault is, therefore, called for. The hostages are exposed to nothing worse than the execution that anyway awaits them, and their lives might even be saved if the rescue mission is successful.

Soft Cops, however, are in a much more difficult position. If the robbers are forced to move first, or to move independently, then they have no alternative but to kill. This produces, as we have seen, kill/stand firm. But both Soft Cops and robbers would rather see don't kill/give in. *This outcome can be achieved by Soft Cops if they move first and give in.* The Soft Cops seize the first move and supply a helicopter to allow the besieged robbers to make their escape. The robbers' response is to free the hostages unharmed. Thus, while the robbers *never* have an incentive to make a quick move, Soft Cops trying to save a roomful of hostages do. They end up rushing to give in in just the same fashion as the freelance victim facing either a pro kidnapper or a pro protection salesperson. This is the only siege scenario that gives the besieged robbers a chance.

The robbers aren't in the clear quite yet, however. An added complication of sieges is that the cops are both the victims and the forces of justice. Worse, they may well face demands that are beyond their control. The robbers may want a plane, for example, and the cops may simply not be able to provide one. At $50 million each, few companies will lend one of their airliners to the cops so that they can let a bunch of bankrobbers go free. Soft Cops may want to give in but will just not be able to. In this case, all they can do is be as nice as possible and hope for the best.

All of this is well illustrated by the case of Lewis Robinson versus the New York Police Department. Robinson was a US sailor facing a disciplinary hearing that concerned a minor theft. He was feeling pretty miserable, not to say paranoid, on the bus back to base and got so angry at the people he thought were staring at him that he shot one of them in the neck. At this point he decided to go 'all the way' and ordered the driver to go to JFK Airport, along with his busload of twenty-three hostages. At the airport he demanded $6 million and a plane by 4 p.m. that afternoon but was immediately encircled by police. He forced one of the passengers to tell the police that if they used tear gas, he would kill as many hostages as he could before the cops got to him. He forced the driver to keep the bus moving.

Soon after this one of the female passengers, a member of the armed services, tried to jump him. He hit her with his gun. The driver stopped the bus to let him force the girl out of the door. As Robinson was doing this, the driver tried to push him out at the same time. Robinson pulled around and shot an old lady. After this the NYPD's world-famous hostage negotiation team arrived on the scene.

They offered Robinson a phone, so that they could negotiate with him. He refused, then he accepted. Nevertheless, he refused to speak directly to the police, forcing another hostage to do this for him. He didn't want the police to know how scared he was.

As the 4 p.m. deadline approached, the police negotiators promised to meet all his demands but stalled for time. They introduced a particularly important piece of negotiation around the deadline time and talked Robinson through it without his realizing. The cops claimed to have the ransom money on the way and to be looking for a plane. Robinson wasn't that interested in the money (he had already offered to share it with the hostages). He asked for the 150–200 police around the bus to pass the hat. He would take whatever they could raise, and they could post on the rest to him later. Nothing much happened.

The cops tried to force the issue by refusing to talk to anyone but Robinson. In response, he shot and wounded another hostage. He then forced the hostage who had been doing the talking to tell the cops that he himself would be shot if they didn't back down. They didn't back down. Robinson forced the hostage to the floor and pretended to shoot him. One of the police negotiators was so distressed by this that he had to be taken off the case.

Finally, at 8.30 p. m. Robinson took the phone himself. He repeated his threat to kill the remaining hostages if he didn't get a plane and as much money as could be raised. Then he threw the phone out of the window. A decoy plane was provided at 8.40 p. m. in a part of the airport reserved for such events and set up for an ambush. Robinson didn't like the look of things and forced a hostage to drive the bus in an attempt to break out of the airport. After a twenty-two minute chase, the bus was finally rammed and disabled.

The police now spoke to Robinson using bull horns. They asked him to surrender on the grounds that he hadn't done anything that was too bad yet. They claimed that he'd have an easier time if he surrendered right away than if he killed any more hostages.

Soon after this he surrendered.

The important point about this particular siege is that *none* of the hostages was shot in response to the failure of the police to comply with threats. Those who died or were injured were either picked out because they tried to overpower Robinson themselves or because he got jumpy and shot them for more or less no reason. The cops did give way when he made specific threats, in line with the NYPD's famous soft line. The one thing that they didn't do was to grant his demands, as much because this was not within their power as because they didn't want to. They might have *wanted* to be Soft Cops, but they were forced to be Tough because they didn't happen to have $6 million and a plane. We'll never know whether they were *really* Soft or Tough because Robinson never really put this to the test. Obsessed with his desire for a plane, which the police couldn't give him, he didn't use his bargaining power to get himself out of trouble.

If he had threatened to kill one hostage for every fifteen minutes that they didn't let him out of the airport and another for every fifteen minutes that they followed him, he would soon have found out just how Tough they were. Soft Cops would have let him go; Tough ones wouldn't. Tough Cops would have mounted a full frontal assault as soon as Robinson had killed his first hostage to demonstrate that he was not bluffing. This highlights the important bargaining leverage that even the possibility of a full frontal assault gives to the police. Robinson had already killed hostages. If he killed a few more and got captured or hurt, things would probably not be any worse for him than they already were. He had no incentive not to carry out his threat, which gave *him* a big bargaining advantage.

Now, the police might claim, and may even believe, that they launch full frontal assaults to save the lives of hostages. But since the abolition of the death penalty, a full frontal assault provides the only way in which a hijacker might end up dead. This is probably the only thing that is worse (and, of course, for some people it may even seem better) than spending a long time in jail for murder. Let's not be coy. The full frontal assault gives the police a chance to kill the robber. By keeping hold of this possibility, the cops get back some of their bargaining leverage. The counter-threat that they offer by implication is 'Kill a hostage and there's a good chance you die too. When we come through that door, who knows what will happen?' The robber now has a reason to spare the hostages, and the cops are back in business.

One thing that the case of Robinson versus the NYPD illustrates very nicely is the importance of communication. When two people are in direct conflict, communication is largely irrelevant. Neither side would believe the other, even if they could communicate. When both sides have some incentive to co-operate (and everyone always prefers that the hostages live *if* the cops give in), communication can be critical. It can be a one-way or a two-way process. A bull horn is a one-way method of communication; I can bellow at you, but you can't answer back. A letter is a one-way method of communication. A kidnapper can send a ransom demand through the mail, but the victim can't reply unless the kidnapper has ill-advisedly included his address. If the kidnapper says that the hostage will be killed if the money isn't in such-and-such place at so-and-so time, then the victim can't try to beat him down. A telephone, on the other hand, is an interesting two-way method of communication. Either party can slam the receiver down whenever he wants to. On the other hand, if you want to talk, you've got to listen.

It's often the case that someone can put himself in a very strong bargaining position if he can talk to the victim but the victim can't talk to him. If a victim can't talk to you, he can't threaten. If he can't threaten, he won't be tempted to carry out the threat he hasn't made. On the other hand, it's almost impossible to do a deal on a bull horn. Coming to terms involves two-way communication. This means that those people who play to win often tend to favour one-way methods of speaking to their victims, while people who want to deal like face-to-face contact, telephones and so forth.

All of this has some interesting implications for siege negotiations. One possible ploy for besieged robbers or hijackers — although this technique has not, to the best of my knowledge, been used to date — is for them to set things up so that only one-way communication is possible. They could, for example, bring along a high-powered public address system. Through this they could play stirring music at a volume loud enough to drown out any bull horn. They could switch off this music only in order to broadcast their demands. The net effect should be to put almost as much pressure on the cops as a threat to start shooting hostages. Soft Cops would have little option but to capitulate. Tough ones would launch a rescue mission.

Robinson used a variation on this strategy when he refused to speak to the police himself and only communicated on the land line through one of the hostages. He could at least give the impression of simply making demands and not listening to the responses. In practice, of course, it is likely that he listened to the messages relayed to him; the result was not as good as a genuine one-way system. This is what he realized when he made his final demand in person, then threw the phone out of the window.

Looking at things from the other side, the bull horn is the trademark of Tough Cops. It enables them to threaten to their heart's content, without ever putting them in the position of even having to *consider* counter-threats. As soon as a land line is installed, the besieged robber can threaten to start shooting hostages, and chinks may appear in the toughest armour. Tough Cops facing a robber with a busload of hostages should consider simply relaying a one-way message that goes: 'In one minute we're coming in. If you don't harm the hostages, you can live. If we hear a single shot, we come in, and we come in hard. You'll probably end up dead.' In practice, this is what happens in a rescue mission. There is no reason not to make this clear to the robber. Denied the opportunity to *threaten* to kill a hostage, actually killing one serves little purpose. It would be a Tough robber indeed who did not submit. The Robinson siege ended, of course, with the cops talking over bull horns and him unable to reply.

This consideration of communication shows that the cops are in better position in sieges than was apparent at first sight. Once they have besieged the robber, they can control the communication. They can offer a land line or they can refuse it. Once the Robber has a land line, he can only throw it out of the window once. After that he must wait until they allow him to have another. The cops can *always* communicate with the robber, using bull horns and other paraphernalia. The robber can always be denied such communication by the cops, unless he has had the foresight to provide himself with a bull horn or a powerful PA system. While you might not always *want* to communicate, the ability to control the channels of communication, and therefore to choose whether you communicate or not, is a considerable advantage in this sort of negotiation.

Nothing can compensate for the fact that when you are a besieged robber, the place you most want to be is home.

Only *very* occasionally does anyone volunteer to take part in a siege, since the best that can be hoped for is to be no worse off than before. Sometimes, as in the case of the Iranian Embassy siege in London, people deliberately get themselves into sieges in order to extract political concessions. These cases are really examples of hijackings and should be treated accordingly. Once we allow for the fact that buildings can be hijacked as well as planes, the siege proper becomes a depressing business and certainly not a source of revenue.

8

Sudden death

Both hijacking and sieges concentrate the mind wonderfully on the subject of sudden death, illustrating the bargaining advantage that can be wielded by someone who doesn't mind dying. However, while posthumous payoffs are important, they are only one aspect of the problem.

Most people don't like the thought of dying. Many don't even consider posthumous payoffs. Nearly everybody tries to avoid doing things that are certainly going to end with a trip to the mortuary. On the other hand, most people want to get rich. Getting rich usually means taking risks. Taking risks usually involves getting into things that *might* end in disaster. A person's attitude to risk is clearly crucial. Those who are prepared to take bigger risks can play for bigger payoffs while still using the same stake.

Two things are important here. In the first place, everyone puts a different value on his or her own life. This may seem a little odd at first sight. You might think that everyone would put an infinite value on staying alive. This cannot be true, however, as everyone takes tiny risks in the course of even a mundane day-to-day existence. Since crossing the road entails some tiny chance that I will be killed by a runaway steamroller, I would never cross the road at all if I valued my life infinitely. Infinity multiplied by anything other than zero, even if it is the smallest number that has ever been invented, is still infinity. (Infinity multiplied by zero is a mess.) Every time I cross the road, therefore, I prove that I put a finite value on my life. I prove that I'm prepared to put it on the line for certain payoffs if the odds are attractive enough.

Every time I cross the road I bet my life, at odds of several million to one on, for the payoff of getting to the other side.

You can easily put this to the test if you have the mind and enough money. Go to the bank and draw out fifty grand in large-denomination notes. Then go into the lobby of a tall building. Find two people who have the same amount of money in their own bank accounts, equally nice houses, equally shiny cars, equally good jobs and so on. Offer fifty grand in large bills to whichever of the two is prepared to jump from the higher floor on to the concrete forecourt. They may both jump from the first floor. Move on to the second. They may both jump. Keep going up. One will probably chicken out before the other. You can make up your own mind whether to pay off the winner or not (this is irrelevant and, with any luck, the winner will not be in a position to collect). Whatever you decide, you will, however, have proved an important point. The winner values his life less than the loser. The payoff is the same for both sides; the odds are the same for both sides; but the loser is not prepared to bet his life for this payoff at those odds, while the winner is. The winner's life must be worth less. He wins (or dies) for precisely this reason.

In the second place, nothing is certain. Worse than this, even when things are uncertain, we are usually uncertain about how uncertain they are. And so on, *ad infinitum*. Otherwise bookies would starve. When I back a horse in the 2.30, I know the odds if I make my bet on the track. What I don't know is the probability of winning. This I guess at. When I think the probability of winning is better than the bookies' odds, I bet. When I think it's worse, I don't. Any other method of betting on horses is a road to ruin. If I guess the real chance of winning correctly, I don't necessarily win my bet, but if I *always* guess correctly, I make money in the long term.

This leads to a paradox: I may know much more about horses than some wild-eyed yobbo in the county stand, yet I still lose, while he wins. He wins by making a bad bet and getting lucky. I lose by making a good bet that doesn't succeed. Say Speedy Gonzales has a 30 per cent chance of winning the race, while Royal Wedding has only a 5 per cent chance. The bookies offer five-to-one on each. They will fix their odds on the basis of how the money is coming in, and in a royal wedding year they take all kinds of money on Royal Wedding from wild-eyed county yobbos. Poor old Speedy is a foreigner and unlikely to attract much action from the county set. I back Speedy Gonzales because this is a good bet. If I always get paid off at five-to-one on bets that have a 30 per cent chance of success, I make money in the long run. Royal Wedding is a mug's bet, and mugs' bets are the bookies' livelihood. But this race is the one-in-twenty that he wins. The yobbos get paid off and go home thinking that it's been a great year for the monarchy. They never realize how stupid they are.

What has all this horse-riding got to do with death? Before I offer an answer, consider a particularly interesting fact about human nature. Human beings can be divided into Optimists and Pessimists. Optimists think that things are probably going to turn out all right, even when they don't really know what the probability of this happening actually is. Pessimists think that exactly the same things are going to turn out quite differently and, indeed, much worse. Optimists will make bets, including bets with their lives, when pessimists will not. They do this because they estimate the real odds in a more generous way.

Just watch any pedestrian crossing. Some people, Optimists, fling themselves across the road almost under the wheels of heavy lorries, buses and even bulldozers. Others, Pessimists, won't go near the kerb if they can see a bicycle half a mile off. Even two people who value their lives equally will behave differently in the face of risk.

The point of all this is that hijackers and besieged robbers make threats that involve betting their lives. Both expose themselves to an acknowledged risk of death. Carrying out such a threat often entails killing a hostage who is their only passport to safety. Carrying out some hijack threats involves suicide. The cops must work out whether these threats are credible. To do this, they will need to decide how much the threatener values his own life and whether he is an optimist or a pessimist. A pessimist who values his life relatively highly will be less likely to expose himself to the risks arising from carrying out the threat than an optimist who values his life cheaply. This makes his threat less credible — and *this* in turn, of course, has far-reaching consequences. If a threat to kill hostages isn't believed by the police, then Soft Cops aren't going to give in, and Tough Cops aren't going to launch a raid. Both of these quick endings are ruled out, and everyone can dig himself in for a long wait.

This, for example, is what happened at the Balcombe Street Siege. The IRA men who holed up in a flat in London's Balcombe Street and held hostage the couple who lived there clearly valued their lives quite highly. Police experience of IRA sieges had shown that none of the perpetrators had willingly put his life on the line. The police took a gamble that the Balcombe Street men would think the same way. They cracked the siege by putting up large screens around the area and bringing in the SAS, which had a reputation for tough responses to incidents like this. The screens enabled the police to tell the IRA men that the SAS were coming in and that the news media would not be able to see what happened. They gave the impression that the hostages were expendable. We will never know whether the SAS would actually have gone in shooting before the hostages had been harmed, but no one was in any doubt that the Army's hard men would play things like the toughest of tough cops. The siege crumbled, and the IRA men surrendered.

The crucial piece of intelligence needed by the police in confrontations like this is to find out how their enemy feels about life. This explains official preoccupation with bugging places where bad guys are holed up. Given this intelligence, the cops are in a much stronger bargaining position. This is a very good reason why hijackers or besieged robbers should never release *any* hostage until the situation has resolved itself. Nearly every police success is built on the basis of knowledge of the bad guys' state of mind. Released hostages can reveal invaluable information about this, even if they have been blindfolded throughout. One solution is for the bad guys not to speak to each other at all but to write down every communication with each other, which will prevent a quaver in the voice from giving away a fading resolve. Not only does the ruse confound police bugs, but it also opens up the possibility of releasing the odd hostage if this should seem desirable. When lives are wagered for high stakes, the last thing that should leak out is the information that the threatener is scared of dying.

The thing that any opponent most wants to know in any negotiation is how you feel about the payoffs. This is always your secret unless you choose to reveal it. When one of the payoffs is your own death, this secret can be your only life-line. One way of keeping the secret is to pass as a lunatic. The psychiatric profession, no doubt, has a range of subtle and sophisticated definitions of lunacy. As far as out-smarting the opposition is concerned, however, there is only one. A lunatic is someone who doesn't think like you, someone who thinks so differently from you that you can't even imagine how he does think. Being a lunatic can be an enormous advantage when it comes to beating the opposition.

I shuffle into the room, produce a sawn-off shotgun from my briefcase and politely insert it into your mouth. I threaten to blow the top off your head if you don't buy me a bottle of beer, and you probably think that I am trying to make a point about threats. You smile and say you understand, but you don't think of buying me a bottle of beer. I seem sane, and you know that I would never think it worthwhile to slaughter you for a bottle of beer. It would cost me more to repaint the ceiling than to buy the beer myself. On the other hand, if I stagger in blasting the pump-action shotgun all around me and foaming at the mouth, if I reek of stale beer and vomit and my eyes are rolling around in their sockets, you may consider the purchase. You will forget about weighing up how sorry I will be if I shoot you against the minor advantage I gain from a free beer. You decide I'm a lunatic and buy me a beer. I win. You may even buy me a beer if I threaten to blow *my own* head off in *your* recently decorated living-room. I win again.

So who said lunatics are crazy? It should by now be quite clear that some lunatics are quite sane. Even a tiny possibility that you might be dealing with a real one may be enough to persuade you, life-loving Pessimist that you are, to back down. This all goes to show that any operator worth his salt should keep the contents of his cranium a closely guarded secret.

Another aspect of death that affects this type of bargaining is its relationship with *trust*. It's very easy to think that trust has no place at all in sieges and hijackings, but this simply isn't so. Most sieges and hijacks are strung out over hours, if not days. Nearly all involve a sequence of moves by the various actors. When any group of actors is involved in a sequence of moves, trust can be critical.

We've already seen that communication lies at the heart of a deal. You can't do a deal if you can't communicate. The real trouble is that you can't believe a thing people say. I've just threatened to blow the top of your head all over my new white ceiling. Since I'm not foaming at the mouth or speaking in tongues, you don't believe me. The only way I can convince you I'm telling the truth is to go ahead and do it. Actions, as they say, speak louder than words. *Then* you'll trust me. The trouble is that unless I meet you again at the Pearly Gates, your trust isn't much use to me. Now, if I'd threatened to redo your cavities with my new electric drill, things would be quite different. If you don't trust me, I pull out my shining Black and Decker and carry out the threat. *Now* you trust me. We can do a deal.

The electric drill trick is the sort of stunt that oils the wheels of the protection business. It's not a lot of use in hijackings and sieges (though anyone setting off on such an undertaking would be well advised to pack a Black and Decker, a chainsaw and one or two other items of trust-enhancing hardware before leaving home). Hijackings and sieges often involve suicide threats, and it's not much good being trusted and dead. Respect is fine, and very valuable too, but it can be carried too far. For the hijackers, the problem is how to build up credibility and still live to use it.

Hijack and siege are sudden-death games. They share with nuclear strike, chicken and a few others the important property that the proceedings are apt to come to an abrupt halt. Usually we play games over and over again and learn from our mistakes. You sell me a second-hand Cadillac convertible and promise me that it's 100 per cent legitimate. Two days later the boys in blue are knocking on my door, and I learn not to trust you. I learn the hard way, but it's not *too* hard, and I live to put the lesson into practice with my electric drill. Like all games, the sudden-death variety can be played over and over. The difference is that this is rather like walking backwards and forwards along a tightrope. No matter if you make it a hundred times, you can still put a foot wrong on the hundredth-and-first trip and be dead in seconds. This means that you can never really trust an opponent in a sudden-death game, however much you might want to or need to. The trust that you can often build up depends upon the chance that you may have to punish a perfidious opponent. If that same opponent can sucker you into sudden death, there's nothing to hold him back, thus no reason for you to trust him.

So you're a robber and you're holed up in some bank. Outside the scenery is infested with police. They tell you that if you don't come out double-quick, they're going to come in and shoot you. They tell you that if you do come out, hands held high, they'll go easy. Why should you believe them? If the TV cameras and a journalist or two are around, then you've got a chance. They may still shoot you, of course, but then no one will trust them the next time. They do have an incentive to keep their word.

But they may say instead that they're coming in anyway, and that if your hands aren't held high when they get there, they're going to let loose. Do you believe them then? They can always come out and tell the journalists that your hands weren't high enough or that you made a move. Even if you don't, there's all that nuisance of going to court, giving evidence, locking you up and so on. It's a lot easier to shoot you. Now you really are playing a sudden-death game; it's just you and the police. You won't have a chance to learn from your mistakes, and you won't have a chance to pay them back. The only way you can even the odds is to let them know straightaway that you'll slaughter as many hostages as possible the moment a policeman comes through the door. This, of course, doesn't make it a two-sided sudden-death game. The police force will live to fight another day whatever you do, but if they rush in and you slaughter a pile of hostages, this will get them into serious trouble. They may rush in anyway, but it's the best you can do. Above all, if you decide to surrender, wait until the TV cameras have arrived and do it in public.

Most sudden-death games are one-sided. You don't often find both players risking death in the same game, though Russian roulette played competitively for high stakes is an obvious exception. You and I each put up a huge stake, place a single bullet in a six-chambered revolver and spin it. We take turns to put the gun to our own head and pull the trigger. The chamber is not spun between shots. Either of us is free to back down at any stage. The winner is either the only survivor or the one who doesn't back down. Would you rather fire first or second?

This is straightforward, though counter-intuitive. The person who shoots first *always* has a smaller chance of being shot than the person who shoots second. If the game goes the distance, then the first to pull the trigger has a one-in-six, then a one-in-four, then a one-in-two chance of dying. The second to pull has a one-in-five, one-in-three and one-in-one chance of dying. *But* the second to pull has the luxury of knowing for certain that he will die on the sixth shot and that he can therefore pull out at that stage, losing only the money. On top of this, the first to shoot may, of course, die with the first shot. Before the first shot is fired, there is a one-in-six chance that the bullet is in any one of the chambers. The second to shoot will never expose himself to more of those one-in-six chances than the first and will often expose himself to one fewer. He will only conceivably have to pull the trigger twice (the second and fourth pulls), while the first to shoot may have to pull three times (the first, third and fifth pulls). Before the game starts, the first to pull takes on an even chance of dying for a bet at even odds. The second to pull takes on a one-in-three chance of dying for a bet at even odds. The counter-intuitive element arises because while it may feel as if you've won when you've pulled the trigger and nothing happens, if fact you've simply not lost. You can never win on your turn. Going second gives you a chance of winning without ever pulling the trigger, and you always win having exposed yourself to less risk than your opponent.

We would have to toss a coin to decide who shot first. It would never be worth your while playing the game if you weren't prepared to die and if I was. In that case, we'd toss the coin and you'd back down for certain if you lost the toss, and you'd back down anyway the five times out of six that I wasn't killed with the first shot, even if you won the toss. You'd have a one-in-twelve chance of winning and would be making an evens bet, a bad business proposition. I, on the other hand, would have an eleven-in-twelve chance of winning and would also be making an evens bet — and that's *good* business. You wouldn't choose to get involved. If we were *forced* to play with each other, my willingness to run a one-in-six risk of death would give me an elevenfold advantage over you.

The point is that in real life people can sometimes force you to play sudden-death games. If they are prepared to stand a little more risk than you are, they can come out miles ahead. This, of course, is why death is the Great Leveller. When you face hopeless odds, a little bet with your life can even them up considerably. You won't want to make a bet like this unless you have a good idea of just how far your opponent will go. This is a matter of practice. Sudden-death games are for experienced operators; there's not much scope for learning on the job.

9

With one leap
he was free

It should not come as much of a surprise to anybody to discover that if you're prepared to kill and you're prepared to die, you can make a lot of money. The huge profits offered by the strategic professions of extortion, kidnap, blackmail, hijack bear this out. Much more important, it is clear that just being prepared to kill or die is usually good enough. Actual killing and actual dying are rarely necessary. One of the threads that sews all of the preceding chapters together is the central importance of credibility, of respect. Once credibility is established, threats are usually sufficient to do the job. Threats, of course, are cheap.

It is quite remarkable, considering how far civilization has progressed in many other fields, that we know so little about credibility. What we do know, we tend to know in our bones and our guts rather than our brains. The people who know most about credibility are usually the people who have solved the problem of how to put it to maximum use. Successful politicians, for example, tend to be successful because people believe their promises, their threats and sometimes both. Both revolutions and repressive dictators can succeed because nobody has fully mastered the secrets of credibility to the point of being able to manufacture it out of nothing. A month's events can turn even the most feared of tyrants into a pathetic fugitive, as credibility suddenly runs like sand through his fingers. On the other hand, to seize power all you need is sufficient muscle to kill key figures in the *ancien régime*, to seize the national broadcasting station and to declare the dawn of a new age. More precisely, all you need is that and credibility. Some try it and succeed; others wind up dead. When someone walks through the door waving a pistol in each hand, it's still pretty hard to pick a winner.

Most of us daily run into showdowns in which we put our credibility on the line. Any car driver, for example, faces them all the time. That pedestrian who has just stepped off the kerb knows that you're coming and knows that you'll have to slow down if you're not going to hit him. He knows you still have time to slow down. He's *daring* you to hit him. But, to set against this, you know that he can still jump out of the way. You know that he knows you know he can still jump out of the way. One of you must back down. If neither does, someone dies, while the other gets into a lot of trouble.

Most drivers are familiar with this confrontation, and most have given in on some occasions while winning on others. They have usually given in facing a pedestrian who looks as if he really means it. They have usually won because they have smelt the pedestrian's lack of credibility, sensed that he is going to jump for safety when the chips are down. (Having a highly developed sense of smell, dogs are experts at assessing credibility. Non-drivers, who are unable to practise on pedestrians and unwilling to practise on motorists, can develop their skills by provoking, and winning, confrontations with ferocious canines.)

Little as we know about credibility in one-off confrontations, we can be quite certain about one thing. In long-running interactions, carrying out threats and promises can only enhance credibility. while breaking promises and backing down from threats can only damage it. This is the key to the much greater profits earned by professional operators in all forms of strategic business. A freelance bank robber is still a bank robber. If he robs a bank, he has still got the money. Bank robbery, like everything else, must be done properly, but there is no built-in disadvantage that undermines the earning potential of the expert freelance. In any occupation that depends upon threats and promises (and politics, blackmail, extortion and kidnapping are prime examples), the professional does have a built-in advantage over a freelance, however expert that freelance might be.

The very fact that a pro is a pro is what produces the extra bargaining leverage. The pro needs credibility or he goes broke. The need for credibility forces him to take a tougher line, often making short-term sacrifices for long-term gain. Thus the professional kidnapper kills the hostage when a freelance would set him free. The pro blackmailer publishes the dirt when a mercenary freelance would throw it away. The professional protection salesman goes out late at night to smash up the premises of recalcitrant nightclub owners when it would be much more fun to stay at home and watch *Dallas* on TV. All of these sacrifices are designed to instil fear and trepidation in future victims. They have nothing at all to do with spite or revenge. Taking it out on those who defy you is simply to encourage the others. The opportunity to work off any malevolent frustration may be welcome but is no more than icing on the cake.

The net result of maintaining a tough reputation is that no one needs to get hurt, since credible threats are rarely enacted. Everybody benefits.

The fact that everybody does indeed benefit from the successful use of a credible threats gives the strategic professions their distinctive character. By 'benefit', I don't really mean that everyone is *happy* with what has happened by the end of the day. What is quite clear, however, is that everyone could easily be *worse* off. If the threat is enacted, the victim gets hurt and the threatener risks punishment. Neither wants this. The victim may wish that the threat had never been made but nevertheless comes to terms to avoid an even worse disaster, which is having the threat carried out. Everybody benefits in the sense that everyone avoids disaster.

The possibility of mutual benefit encourages co-operation. In this very real sense, professional kidnapper and victim co-operate to save the life of the hostage. The demand is reasonable, so the victim is prepared to pay if paying guarantees release. The kidnapper, concerned with credibility, will be forced to kill the hostage if no money is forthcoming. Both sides want to avoid kill/no pay in favour of pay/no kill and, with effective co-operation, they can succeed. Such co-operation extends not only to producing a satisfactory outcome to the negotiations but also to collaborating to keep the police out of things. One of the tremendous advantages that strategic crime maintains over other forms of crime is the fact that the chances of apprehension and punishment *must* be lower, since many victims will not involve the police and will even be quite obstructive if the police involve themselves.

The fact that both sides often want to deal raises the problem of enforcement. Since neither side trusts the other, and since it is often inappropriate to involve the straight enforcement industry, a lucrative role emerges for the professional. Professional enforcers will trade on their credibility, transforming credibility directly into cash by way of fees for enforcement contracts. The role of enforcer or stakeholder, therefore, can be the most lucrative in the business.

When deals aren't possible, either because no middle-man is available or because the two sides are not united in preferring an alternative outcome, the victim can often be forced to co-operate by being given the first move. Strictly speaking, the notion of a dominant strategy, a strategy that is better regardless of the opponent's chosen course of action, is only relevant when both players move independently or simultaneously. In reality, most games either offer the players moves in sequence or the option of moving at will. When all players have a dominant strategy, the order of the moves does not affect the result. When some players do not have dominant strategies, this means, by definition, that their best moves depend upon the moves made by the other players. This in turn means that the player with a dominant strategy may be forced *not* to choose that strategy. In this sense, such a player is forced to act against what might appear, superficially, to be in his best interest. Thus the kidnap victim's dominant strategy is no pay, yet he rushes to move, and to pay, when confronted by a pro kidnapper. It is the fact that the pro kidnapper has no dominant strategy that gives him his bargaining advantage.

In all of this, the key difference between strategic crime and common-or-garden crime is the fact that committing a criminal act does no more than give the strategic operator a bargaining advantage that still needs to be exploited. The common-or-garden criminal gets a payoff from the crime itself. The more direct nature of the payoff for a bank robbery must, however, be offset against the increased chance of capture (since the victim has every incentive to call the cops) and the generally safer conditions created by the arm's-length nature of many strategic negotiations.

In this, the penultimate paragraph, we must return to the subject of death. Death is, in many ways, rather like infinity. As we have noted, if you multiply anything (except nothing) by infinity, you get infinity. If you divide anything (except nothing) by infinity, you get nothing. This is an enormously valuable certainty, which can nevertheless leave you feeling that you don't quite know where you stand. Threatening to kill people (such as hostages) can perk up expectations, even when the probability of success is very small. The trouble is that death threats are cheap. Making a cheap threat to kill you if you don't pay me an expensive ransom is rather like multiplying infinity by zero. You may rate the chances of losing pretty slim if you decide to face me down. Yet the costs of losing are enormous. If you want to decide whether to back Cheap Thrill to win in the 3.30, the sums are quite simple and their results unambiguous. If you're betting on me to withdraw from a death threat, the sums might be simple, but they don't help much. In the last analysis, it is much more useful to be able to smell weakness than to have a whole building full of computers.

The day they teach computers to smell is the day they might sell one to a blackmailer.